STAND UP POETRY

STAND UP POETRY

AN EXPANDED ANTHOLOGY

Edited by Charles Harper Webb

University of Iowa Press · Iowa City

POETRY

University of Iowa Press, Iowa City 52242

Design by Richard Hendel

http://www.uiowa.edu/~uipress

The publication of this book was generously supported
by the University of Iowa Foundation.

Printed on acid-free paper

Library of Congress
Cataloging-in-Publication Data
Stand Up poetry: an expanded anthology / edited by
Charles Harper Webb.
p.   cm.
ISBN 0-87745-795-6
1. American poetry—California—Los Angeles.
2. American poetry—20th century.   3. Recitations.
I. Webb, Charles Harper.
PS572.L6 S83 2002
811'.5408097494—dc21

                              2001054277

CONTENTS

....

STAND UP POETRY: AN UPDATE

. . . .

Back in the 1970s, while editing *Madrona* magazine in Seattle, I began to notice, popping up here and there, a kind of witty, sometimes sexy, often gritty, outrageous, and iconoclastic poetry far removed from the Roethke-influenced nature poems that surrounded me in the Northwest. The best of this new poetry showed insight, imagination, craft, emotional power, and philosophical depth, but most of all, it was funny, and it was fun.

Edward Field and Billy Collins in New York, Russell Edson in Connecticut, and Philip Dacey in the Midwest were all writing what I would later call Stand Up poems. The major concentration of this poetry, though, seemed to be in southern California. When I came to teach at California State University, Long Beach, in 1984, this poetry was going strong. As a result, a large number of people—not just in the university, but in the community at large—bought books of poetry, went to readings, and in general supported the art.

In 1987, I wrote an essay describing the poetry at the center of this rich cultural scene. Titled "Five Stand Up Poets," the essay used the work of southern California poets Ron Koertge, Gerald Locklin, Suzanne Lummis, Laurel Ann Bogen, and Elliot Fried to define what I believed to be a distinct and important movement in American poetry. After presentation as the 1988 Phi Beta Kappa University Lecture at CSULB, the essay was revised and published in the *Chiron Review* and then rewritten as the introduction to *Stand Up Poetry: The Poetry of Los Angeles and Beyond* (Red Wind Books, 1990).

A lot has changed since then. Joseph Epstein's 1988 essay "Who Killed Poetry?"[1] set off a fire storm in the poetry community by pronouncing contemporary American poetry, for all intents and purposes, irrelevant. Epstein and his ideas were widely excoriated; still, some readers cheered to have the elephant-in-the-poetry-room finally acknowledged. In certain quarters, there had long been a sense that, by its teaching and the poetry it produced, the Academy was, if not killing, at least seriously harming American poetry. Dana Gioia's "Can Poetry Matter?" (May 1991)[2] heaped fuel on Epstein's flames by agreeing that American poetry's cultural situation was dire. Gioia, though, offered a plan for recovery. This plan emphasized, among other things, effective performance.

Nationwide, performance poetry—much of it overtly antiliterary—was experiencing an upsurge in popularity. Coffeehouses were springing up and hosting poetry readings as in beatnik days. Within a few years, poetry "slams" were ubiquitous, bringing excitement, rowdiness, sleaze, and game-show competition to an activity that had previously been characterized, for the most part, by decorum and restraint. *Poet* proved to be an attractive pop-culture identity (and required less writing than *novelist*). A soulful art in a world seen as increasingly soulless, poetry attained such high status among the young and hip that it was actually used in ads for jeans. Bill Moyers produced two well-received television shows—*The Power of the Word*, and *Fooling with Words*—for PBS. These, and their companion books, made use of Stand Up poetry, as did PBS's *The United States of Poetry*, which added music and extra pictures to the mix. Movies were made about poetry slams.

At the same time, the growing number of university writing programs presented more and more poetry readings. And the more readings, the greater the need for poems that worked well when read aloud. No one likes to bomb onstage. Consequently, aspects of performance poetry—humor, natural language, edgy subject matter, strong and overt emotion—began to filter into mainstream "literary" poetry. Inside the Academy and out, there was a general (although not universal) movement away from the dour and the daunting toward more accessible, reader-friendly poetry.

Exactly why all of this happened when it did is a subject for another book, or books. Whatever the reasons, mainstream poetry has, in the past fifteen years, moved much closer to the Stand Up aesthetic. In a sense, mainstream poetry has absorbed Stand Up in the way that a large tribe absorbs a smaller one, intermingling genes. Some younger poets—emerging from the slam and performance scenes, or influenced by them—have written Stand Up poetry over their entire careers. But veteran poets are writing it too.

The term *Stand Up poetry* has entered the lexicon, although it is interpreted in many ways. A friend once told me: "I know what Stand Up is. It's like the Greatest Hits." He meant that Stand Up poems are those for which poets get the most requests. This isn't always true, but the qualities of Stand Up poems do make them ideal for oral presentation, as well as for enjoyable silent reading.

So what are those qualities? What exactly is Stand Up poetry?

The term *Stand Up poet* was coined by CSULB professors Gerald Locklin and Charles Stetler to describe Edward Field, whose book *Stand Up, Friend, with Me* was the Lamont Poetry Selection for 1962 and put the nose of the academic establishment severely out of joint.

The term emphasizes a characteristic which has sometimes caused this poetry to be dismissed: its sense of humor. *Stand Up* brings to mind *comic*, a quality that is still anathema in some poetic circles. But the phrase implies more than comedy. Stand Up poems work well when read aloud—when the poet stands up and performs. In addition, the term implies honesty, courage, straightforwardness, as in "stand up for your rights," "stand up and be counted," "stand up for what you believe." Like the proverbial "stand up guy," Stand Up poetry is honest, unpretentious, strong.

Because it uses the vernacular, Stand Up poetry is sometimes lumped with "street" poetry of an antiliterary bent. This is a mistake. A good Stand Up poem requires as much literary art as any other good poem.

Stand Up poetry has also been confused with performance art, which may contain elements of poetry but is written primarily to be performed. Stand Up poetry is written for the printed page, bearing in mind that poetry has always been an oral art, at its best when read aloud.

Literary influences on Stand Up poetry encompass all of literature—Aristophanes to Shakespeare, Cervantes to Rabelais to Baudelaire. More recent influences include Walt Whitman, T. S. Eliot, Ezra Pound, Pablo Neruda, Nicanor Parra, W. C. Williams, Karl Shapiro, Dylan Thomas, and Sylvia Plath. The beat poets are clear precursors of Stand Up poetry. Allen Ginsberg's "Howl," Gregory Corso's "Marriage," and Lawrence Ferlinghetti's "Underwear" can all be considered proto–Stand Up poems. The New York School—Frank O'Hara, Kenneth Koch, and even John Ashbery—influenced Stand Up poetry, too.

Just as the influences of Stand Up are diverse, so are the styles of those who write it. Stand Up poetry ranges from expansive to spare, rhapsodic to controlled, surreal to very real. Although this anthology groups writers of Stand Up poems together, Stand Up poetry is not a philosophy or school, and inclusion in this book does not confer membership in any club. Many fine poets who are not included also write Stand Up poems; poets who are included don't always write Stand Up poems.

The first Stand Up anthology focused mainly on poets from southern California. This updated collection preserves a strong core of poets with So-Cal ties, but Stand Up seeds have sprouted everywhere.

I don't claim that any single quality is unique to Stand Up poetry. Nor do I claim that every Stand Up poem contains each of the qualities discussed below. I do believe, however, that the unique combination of the following qualities characterizes Stand Up poetry.

HUMOR

Not every Stand Up poem is fall-down funny, but many make skillful use of humor. Playful, irreverent, and high-spirited, these poems employ the techniques of comedy: timing, absurdity, hyperbole. Stand Up poems frequently display a youthful, rebellious energy, a disconcerting frankness, a love of deflating the pompous and stodgy. A favorite Stand Up technique is to juxtapose the grand with the banal. In Ron Koertge's "All Suffering Comes from Attachment," Buddha's wisdom is applied to the penis.

Ours is an age in which Aristotle's ranking of tragedy as superior to comedy seems more and more suspect. Like other contemporary artists, Stand Up poets use humor as a device ideally suited to capturing the absurdities, enormities, and pathos of modern life.

PERFORMABILITY

To work optimally when read aloud, a poem must be not only dramatic, but understandable—at least on some level—the first time through. This fact has led some critics to dismiss performable poetry as inferior art. Yet Karl Shapiro writes, "If there is only one law of art, it is that the work must be capable of apprehension as a whole and at once . . . like a tree or a woman."[5]

Stand Up poetry embodies this law. In addition, many writers of Stand Up poems perform their work with flair. Although some contemporary poets pride themselves on a flat reading style, insisting that anything other than bare, uninflected words is dishonest, most writers of Stand Up poems disagree. Many have stage experience as actors, dancers, or musicians and enjoy dramatizing their poetry. Some read with the fury of a Medea; some with the timing of a headliner at The Comedy Store. Occasionally, they sing or dance or pantomime.

The best writers of Stand Up poems want these poems to work equally well when read silently or aloud—on the page or on the stage. In person or in print, these poets aren't ashamed to entertain. Yet good Stand Up poems stand up to close reading, too.

CLARITY

Almost all of the best writers have prized clarity, and the best literature is almost always clear.

Stand Up poetry doesn't use verbal smoke screens to disguise lack of content or to avoid revelations about the poets' lives. Stand Up poetry does not require a literary cryptographer to discover its meaning. The profundity of a Stand Up poem is measured not by its difficulty of penetration, but by the depth of its psychological resonance and emotional truth.

NATURAL LANGUAGE

Stand Up poetry embodies Wordsworth's famous dictum that poetry should be written in the language people actually use—that is, the vernacular.

Stand Up poems may embody Pound's advice to "make it new" by rethinking cliché, finding new meaning and vitality in the stale phrases and perceptions that loom large in everyday conversations and lives.

Skillful writers of Stand Up poems accept Yeats's premise that if the poet's work is visible, it's wasted. These poets work with such craft that their poems may seem spontaneous, scarcely crafted at all.

Although the language of Stand Up poems is often rich, metaphoric, and musical, it tends to avoid devices that heighten artificiality. Some Stand Up poems break lines on "weak" words such as *the* or *and*; others take the form of prose, further breaking down poetic formality. Prose poems frequently qualify as Stand Up poetry.

In language as in other areas, Stand Up poetry avoids the arcane in favor of the earthy and accessible.

FLIGHTS OF FANCY

Stand Up poems often create bizarre and outrageous alternative worlds. These unrestrained imaginative flights may jar some sensibilities, but it is a healthy jarring—an urging away from the crabbed and ponderous toward creativity, spontaneity, enthusiasm, and childlike joy. Poetry, as Thoreau said, should strike off chains, not clamp on more.

A STRONG INDIVIDUAL VOICE

Good Stand Up poetry is never what Donald Hall has labeled the "McPoem": interchangeable fodder for undistinguishable literary magazines. Stand Up poems don't deal with neutral subjects in obscure language on the theory that what can't be pinned down can't be faulted. Stand Up poems do not try to mute the writer's voice or submerge the writer's ego. They are not jewellike word clusters without heart or guts. They are not afraid to sound like the product of distinct and highly individual minds.

The best Stand Up poems speak with readers person to person, heart to heart.

EMOTIONAL PUNCH

For millennia, the lyric poem was the literary vehicle of choice for emotional expression. Even today, in the popular mind, poetry is synonymous with emotion. In recent years, however—fearing to fall into triteness, sentimentality, and self-revelation—many poets have pulled back from open and overt expressions of feeling. Poet and critic Steve Kowit declares that much of late twentieth-century verse can be characterized by "its debilitating preference for the tepid, mannered, and opaque."[4]

Stand Up poems, even the funny ones, are not too cool to emote, not too bright and learned to deal directly with strong emotion.

A CLOSE RELATIONSHIP TO FICTION

Many writers of Stand Up poetry are accomplished fiction writers, and Stand Up poems freely use techniques of fiction—conflict, hooks, reversals, character development, dialogue—to grab the reader's attention and hold on. Becoming involved in a story and finding out what happens next are among the pleasures available to readers of Stand Up poems.

USE OF URBAN AND POPULAR CULTURE

Historically, poets have been preoccupied with nature. Like most people born in the United States over the past fifty years, though, writers of Stand Up poetry are mainly city bred. The imagery most natural to them is not meadows and woods, lakes and star-filled skies, but parking lots and smog, supermarkets, freeways, malls, and fast-food stands. Just as nature poetry uses the countryside, Stand Up poetry uses the city as a backdrop against which larger human issues stand revealed. Stand Up poems may satirize the modern world and popular culture, but they glorify it too.

As far back as the late 1950s, Karl Shapiro decried the "sickness of modern poetry," declaring: "It is notable that every art in the twentieth century except poetry has drawn richly from jazz, the movies, advertising, the comic strip, commercial design, and even radio and

TV. Poetry is somehow deprived of its contact with contemporary art on the popular and even commercial levels."[5]

Stand Up poetry has more than made contact. It is full of references to movies, cartoon characters, sports heroes, ads—the mythology of our age. Writers of Stand Up poems use our culture's icons, as poets have always done, to dramatize and illuminate.

WIDE OPEN SUBJECT MATTER

A story, possibly apocryphal, has former Poet Laureate Mark Strand remarking how tired he was of poems about grandfathers and relatives. "Why doesn't someone write a poem about linoleum?" he asked.

What he wanted sounds like a Stand Up poem.

At a time when many writers and editors seem terrified of appearing unseemly—and, therefore, write poems that are understated, distant, and detached—Stand Up poets dare to be rambunctious, excitable, immoderate. They celebrate the visceral: death and sex and love and body functions. Glorying in the fact that people eat and drink and defecate and bleed, they open themselves to personal criticism, not merely quibbles about technique. They risk irking, upsetting, frightening, and offending, by telling unpopular truths about the world and unflattering truths about themselves.

Titles such as Elliot Fried's "Wordsworth's Socks," Thomas Lux's "'I Love You Sweatheart,'" and Gerald Locklin's "Do you remember the scene in *The Godfather* where James Caan says, 'Now make sure that the gun gets stashed in the rest room—I don't want my kid brother walking out of there with nothing but his dick in his hand?'" may at first glance seem silly, dirty, and flippant—unpoetic as linoleum. But writers of Stand Up poems take seriously the fact that the majority of people's lives are spent far removed from the sublime. They embrace the ridiculous, the banal, the vulgar, the embarrassing, and the commonplace, and find poetry waiting there.

FINAL COMMENTS

Although Stand Up poetry has gained a measure of mainstream acceptance, it still has its detractors. Not everyone in the poetry world sees clarity and natural language as virtues. Not everyone applauds accessibility. Humor in poetry is not rare today, but it remains suspect—a second- or third-class citizen. Nonetheless, history often reverses the aesthetic judgments of the times. And Stand Up has one undeniable strength: lots of people—even non-poets—like it.

The inevitable criticism of popular art, of course, is that it lowers standards and abdicates responsibility in order to court the masses. Opera, the novel, theater, and cinema were all, at one time, condemned for the crime of being widely enjoyed. "People love hack writers," goes the argument, "but that doesn't make them good."

True. But the fact that people like Stand Up poetry doesn't make it bad. Entertainment isn't always art, but the best art always entertains, while the worst struggles self-consciously to edify.

Speaking of the need to rescue poetry from "among our duties" and to restore it "to our pleasures," Philip Larkin quotes English novelist Samuel Butler: "I should like to like Schumann's music better than I do; I dare say I could make myself like it better if I tried; but I do not like having to try to make myself like things; I like things that make me like them at once and no trying at all."[6]

Obviously, Stand Up is not the only worthy poetry; nor is it the only poetry I like. But I love the poems in this anthology. Each is the kind I want to show my friends, proclaiming "You've got to read this" and waving the poem in their faces until they do.

The poems in this book were written over a considerable range of years. Some of the oldest are Stand Up classics, which define the genre and yet remain as fresh as the day they were written. Others, although not their author's most recent work, are tried-and-true. I've taught them often, and they always please. Still other poems were written more recently.

As editor, my goal has been to collect the best Stand Up poems that I can find while remaining well aware that any anthology is the result of a series of subjective choices by a person (or people) whose knowledge of the field is necessarily limited and who must inevitably, for many reasons, exclude far more than he or she includes. The size of each poet's selection here implies no judgment about the poet's relative worth.

I don't claim to present a representative sample of any poet's work. I hope readers will seek out more work by those contributors whose poems they enjoy. (And I believe that will be every one of them.)

When I first started to write, I dreamed of converting the whole country to poetry. I've mostly given up that dream. Yet I continue to believe that many more Americans could enjoy poetry than currently do. For this to happen, we need more poems that people will like to read with "no trying at all." This anthology collects that kind of poetry and places it where it will do the most good, reader: in your hands.

Charles Harper Webb

1. Joseph Epstein, "Who Killed Poetry?" *AWP Chronicle* 21 (May 1989): 1–10.

2. Dana Gioia, "Can Poetry Matter?" in *Can Poetry Matter? Essays on Poetry and American Culture* by Dana Gioia (St. Paul: Graywolf Press, 1992): 1–24.

3. Karl Shapiro, *In Defense of Ignorance* (New York: Random House, 1960): 281.

4. Steve Kowit, *The Maverick Poets: An Anthology* (Santee, California: Gorilla Press, 1988): 2.

5. Shapiro, 281–82.

6. Philip Larkin, *Required Writing: Miscellaneous Pieces, 1955–1982* (New York: Farrar, Straus, Giroux, 1982): 82.

STAND
UP
POETRY

······································

FOR DESIRE *Kim Addonizio*

Give me the strongest cheese, the one that stinks best;
and I want the good wine, the swirl in crystal
surrendering the bruised scent of blackberries,
or cherries, the rich spurt in the back
of the throat, the holding it there before swallowing.
Give me the lover who yanks open the door
of his house and presses me to the wall
in the dim hallway, and keeps me there until I'm drenched
and shaking, whose kisses arrive by the boatload
and begin their delicious diaspora
through the cities and small towns of my body.
To hell with the saints, with the martyrs
of my childhood meant to instruct me
in the power of endurance and faith,
to hell with the next world and its pallid angels
swooning and sighing like Victorian girls.
I want this world. I want to walk into
the ocean and feel it trying to drag me along
like I'm nothing but a broken bit of scratched glass,
and I want to resist it. I want to go
staggering and flailing my way
through the bars and back rooms,
through the gleaming hotels and the weedy
lots of abandoned sunflowers and the parks
where dogs are let off their leashes
in spite of the signs, where they sniff each
other and roll together in the grass, I want to
lie down somewhere and suffer for love until
it nearly kills me, and then I want to get up again
and put on that little black dress and wait
for you, yes you, to come over here
and get down on your knees and tell me
just how fucking good I look.

WHAT THE DEAD FEAR *Kim Addonizio*

On winter nights, the dead
see their photographs slipped
from the windows of wallets,
their letters stuffed in a box
with the clothes for Goodwill.
No one remembers their jokes,
their nervous habits, their dread
of enclosed places.
In these nightmares, the dead feel
the soft nub of the eraser
lightening their bones. They wake up
in a panic, go for a glass of milk
and see the moon, the fresh snow,
the stripped trees.
Maybe they fix a turkey sandwich,
or watch the patterns on the TV.
It's all a dream anyway.
In a few months
they'll turn the clocks ahead,
and when they sleep they'll know the living
are grieving for them, unbearably lonely
and indifferent to beauty. On these nights
the dead feel better. They rise
in the morning, refreshed, and when the cut
flowers are laid before their names
they smile like shy brides. Thank you,
thank you, they say. You shouldn't have,
they say, but very softly, so it sounds
like the wind, like nothing human.

GOING TO NORWAY *Jack Anderson*

. . . .

I asked my parents,
"Have you ever thought
of going to Norway?
You are Andersons
and deserve to know
Norway, where we all began.
Do you not wonder
how things are in Norway?
I know that I wonder."
And my parents said,
                              "Yes,
we shall go to Norway,
we are Andersons
and want to see where
our people began.
We are growing old:
we must go now."
                              Yet they stayed
on the dock, staring
at the water
as ship after ship
sailed toward the north,
toward Norway.
                    So I said
to my parents, "Now,
you must leave now.
These are the boats
that are leaving for Norway.
It is not long
or far."
                    Then my parents said,
"Yes, we want to see
Norway: we are Andersons.
But it is so far."
                    They stayed
where they were, watching
the boats leave for Norway
and trying to picture it,

even testing a few words
of that dear language
on their tongues
                        —but standing
still, never moving,
never climbing aboard,
though I kept pleading,
"Please, now, you must leave now
if you want to see Norway."
"Norway?" they murmured,
"Norway? Ah, where is that?"
They stood very still,
grayness crept through their hair;
it frightened me to see them
growing so old,
for I had not thought
such a thing possible.
At last I said,
                        "I must go
to Norway. I am
an Anderson
and want to know
where all of us began.
I must go now."
                        They stood
on the dock, waving
out at the water, and I
waved back over the water
which darkened between us
with distance and tears.

THE HOUSEWIFE *Ginger Andrews*

sits on her carefully made bed.
Her blue curtains are more than half drawn.
All household members are acting perfectly rational.
So everyone is a little boring.
So everyone is a little crazy.
She could pick up
her somewhat expensive marble-based candelabra—
and throw it out her window
because she's bored,
because she's just a little crazy.
For any one of a hundred reasons,
she could throw it.
But she won't.
She'll straighten the bed covers
and, maybe, later,
she'll burn the hell out of dinner.

my sister and I
both wound up back in Coos Bay,
basket cases, lonely as hell.
She was recovering from drugs and alcohol,
I was newly divorced, a Sunday School teacher
with no job skills whatsoever
and two little boys to feed,
praying for a maid job at Best Western.
Lord how we prayed

walking from one end
of Sunset Beach to the other, barefoot,
freezing in tank tops and cutoffs,
hair and makeup perfect,
fingernails painted with three coats
of Wet 'n' Wild, hoping
some good looking single doctor
was walking his dog nearby
should one of us happen
to slice our foot on beach glass.

she's looking for a man physically
and/or mentally abused as a child.
He has a sad but sexy smile,
long eyelashes,
and wears Levis exclusively.
He works hard
when he works.
He draws maximum unemployment benefits
whenever he's laid off. He has been
married two or three times, is currently
behind on his child support payments
but should be back working any day,
plans to get caught up,
is good in bed,
smokes pot, drinks beer, does drugs,
presently has no transportation,
and is obviously in need of a good home-
cooked meal.
She's looking, she says,
for a sick man.
The sicker, the better.

PRAYER *Ginger Andrews*

God bless the chick in Alaska
who took in my sister's ex,
an abusive alcoholic hunk.
Bless all borderline brainless ex-cheerleaders
with long blonde hair, boobs,
and waists no bigger around than a coke bottle
who've broken up somebody else's home.
Forgive my thrill
should they put on seventy-five pounds,
develop stretch marks, spider veins,
and suffer through endless days of deep depression.

Bless those who remarry on the rebound.
Bless me and all my sisters;
the ball and chain baggage
we carried into our second marriages.
Bless my broken brother and his live-in.
Grant him SSI. Consider
how the deeper the wounds in my family,
the funnier we've become.
Bless those who've learned to laugh at what's longed for.
Keep us from becoming hilarious.
Bless our children.
Bless all our exes,
and bless the fat chick in Alaska.

AT 4:00 A.M. ASLEEP *John Balaban*

I wanted to shoot the jerk
whining his wheels on an ice patch
dragging me from sleep
even before sparrows screech the dawn
up from snow-crusted choirs of forsythia
between houses somehow asleep.
But maybe the jerk is a her not a him
some poor drudge who's finally had it
after a long night of shouts and slaps.

Maybe this suburb isn't the dead zone.
Maybe others are awake . . . some old guy
sitting up with arthritis, chain-smoking,
or a mother, leaning over a crib
stroking her child crackling with phlegm,
or some man fishing in a toilet bowl
as his wife sobs into her hands and he spoons up
the blood clot, the embryo sac, to take to the doctor
to see what went wrong.
                              Thinking these things
before falling back to sleep, I realized
I was called out into a field of compassion
into a universe of billions of souls, and
that was a messenger now driving away.

WORDS FOR MY DAUGHTER *John Balaban*

About eight of us were nailing up forts
in the mulberry grove behind Reds's house
when his mother started screeching and
all of us froze except Reds—fourteen, huge
as a hippo—who sprang out of the tree so fast
the branch nearly bobbed me off. So fast,
he hit the ground running, hammer in hand,
and seconds after he got in the house

9

we heard thumps like someone beating a tire
off a rim   his dad's howls the screen door
banging open   Saw   Reds barreling out
through the tall weeds towards the highway
the father stumbling after his fat son
who never looked back across the thick swale
of teazel and black-eyed susans until it was safe
to yell fuck you at the skinny drunk
stamping around barefoot and holding his ribs.

Another time, the Connelly kid came home to find
his alcoholic mother getting raped by the milkman.
Bobby broke a milkbottle and jabbed the guy
humping on his mom. I think it really happened
because none of us would loosely mention that
wraith of a woman who slippered around her house
and never talked to anyone, not even her kids.
Once a girl ran past my porch
with a dart in her back, her open mouth
pumping like a guppy's, her eyes wild.
Later that summer, or maybe the next,
the kids hung her brother from an oak.
Before they hoisted him, yowling and heavy
on the clothesline, they made him claw the creekbank
and eat worms. I don't know why his neck didn't snap.

Reds had another nickname you couldn't say
or he'd beat you up: "Honeybun."
His dad called him that when Reds was little.

———————

So, these were my playmates. I love them still
for their justice and valor and desperate loves
twisted in shapes of hammer and shard.
I want you to know about their pain
and about the pain they could loose on others.
If you're reading this, I hope you will think,
Well, my Dad had it rough as a kid, so what?
If you're reading this, you can read the news
and you know that children suffer worse.

———————

Worse for me is a cloud of memories
still drifting off the South China Sea,
like the 9-year old boy, naked and lacerated,
thrashing in his pee on a steel operating table
and yelling "Dau. Dau," while I, trying to translate
in the mayhem of Tet for surgeons who didn't know
who this boy was or what happened to him, kept asking
"Where? Where's the pain?" until a surgeon
said "Forget it. His ears are blown."

———————

I remember your first Hallowe'en
when I held you on my chest and rocked you,
so small your toes didn't touch my lap
as I smelled your fragrant peony head
and cried because I was so happy and because
I heard, in no metaphorical way, the awful chorus
of Soeur Anicet's orphans writhing in their cribs.
Then the doorbell rang and a tiny Green Beret
was saying trick-or-treat and I thought *oh oh*
but I remembered it was Hallowe'en and where I was.
I smiled at the evil midget, his map-light and night
paint, his toy knife for slitting throats, said,
"How ya doin', soldier?" and, still holding you asleep
in my arms, gave him a Mars Bar. To his father
waiting outside in fatigues I hissed, "You, shit,"
and saw us, child, in a pose I know too well.

I want you to know the worst and be free from it.
I want you to know the worst and still find good.
Day by day, as you play nearby or laugh
with the ladies at Peoples Bank as we go around town
and I find myself beaming like a fool,
I suspect I am here less for your protection
than you are here for mine, as if you were sent
to call me back into our helpless tribe.

BAD JOKE *Dorothy Barresi*

Death says to the darkness, hey, buddy,
I've got an itch.
Come here and scratch my headstone.

Alright, alright,
what's really bothering me
is my mother.

Since she died,
people tell me, buck up,
she sees you,

as if that were a comfort.
I mean, what are we talking about here?
Omniscient J. Edgar

Mother like the worst
nightmare of childhood?
The one where you have your pinafore

hiked up to Maine
and little Johnny Kingston
with his hands somewhere down in Erie, PA

and it feels good
it feels good
and just then your mother clicks in on

high heels of aghast,
where did I go wrong,
dear God wait until I get you home

young lady, arm jerk,
hand holding your hand so high
above your head.

It isn't fair.
All those years cossetting
the little marijuana seeds,

one for each birth control pill
tipped from the
dial-a-clock.

The elaborate ruses, evasions,
the sins that make us
who we are:

we are not her.
Mother, stop bugging me!
These wire taps,

these thick manila files.
All heaven full of mothers
at floaty, star-case cubicles

with earphones
and high-powered telescopes
pointed down, and wicked grins.

GLASS DRESS *Dorothy Barresi*

Lily St. Cyr is dead.
A de-luxe woman,
stripper extraordinaire.
Blonde, like the cortex of a blazing sun
finding the perfect grammar of its form
in sublime asymmetry,
gams and hips and prodigious rolling ass and elegant
poses for the ghost boys newly back from hell
in 1945,
to sit trembling in the old
ghost palaces of burlesque.

Lily St. Cyr is dead.
No tassel-twirling, minimum wage girl.
No discount moon,
no languishing feminine ruses.
She teases the illimitable body,
Marilyn before Marilyn,
Jayne before Jayne.
What she does not do: sing dirty, cootch, or kiss bald heads.
She never takes off
more than she has on.
Lily St. Cyr is dead. Not another bombshell,

but a real atom smasher
dressed up like Salome or the Jungle Maiden
faking love with a parrot,
which gets her arrested at Ciro's,
but who cares?
No one gets hurt here.
Ask the band, those be-bop gods of insect cool, playing
"Say It Isn't So,"
what the difference is
between naked and undressed.
They know with a terrible clarity.

Her generating curves,
her spirals,

her vector rotation of planes and on-stage bubble baths
are the swellest immorality for those
wrecked and crippled boys
in the front row.
Lily St. Cyr is dead.
Knock back a whisky. Dim the spot.
Sweep the dressing room free of parrots, sequins, idolaters.
The Gaiety, the Savoy, the Palace,
the Republic are gone,

and in their place,
vast warehouses of exhausted capital
are erected downtown.
Lily St. Cyr is dead.
The high zero,
the unabashed,
the lithe and swift-leaping—"That's it, boys,
you're not getting any more from me."
Miss Liberty with her bare breasts
striking us dumb! Quick,

before the cops come to shut this show down,
watch her hold up a corner of red velvet curtain
to cover her well-turned
female dexterity.
With a wink and a smile, she is
an ecdysiast of the highest order, "ecdysis" meaning "shedding"
or "nothing." It's true.
In the end, moaning,

we make our sexual pledge of allegiance.
Shed of shame,
we are mad for anything
made of blue lights and such blood.
But the GIs are crying.
They hide their faces, they disturb the air—
what good are their eyes
now that they've seen
what they've seen?
The house lights roar up like rockets for nothing.
Lily St. Cyr is dead.

BLAZON *Dinah Berland*

—In Memory of Helen Berland

My mother with her long, dangling earrings
With her elephant-ear sponges and magnifying mirrors
With her dusty catalogs in boxes
With her fashion magazines
With her sable-hair brushes
With nudes and trumpets in her trompe l'oeil paintings
My mother with her mink jacket and lipstick kisses
With her cigarette holder and beehive hairdo
With her dressmaker's dummy
With her boutique charge accounts
My mother who designed pinafores and submarine insignia
With her plunging necklines and Florida tan
With her party games and piano music
With her lucky queen of hearts laughter
My mother who sang "Nature Boy" and cried
With her fear of strangers, chills, and natural disasters
My mother who amazed her doctors for sixteen years
And said her last words, "She did a good job,"
When I held up her painting of a ballerina in the clouds
My mother who insisted I keep her age a secret, even
On her headstone, and hated her face
In the mirror at the hospice
A mask of wax stretched across her cheekbones
With her breathing like a freight train, like a feather
With her hand turning blue as it clutched mine
My mother with her paintings of brilliant birds
With her secret life as a dancer

I EAT LUNCH WITH A SCHIZOPHRENIC *Laurel Ann Bogen*

I check for gestapo agents
under the table
there are no electronic bugs
in the flowers
We talk freely
about jamming devices
and daredevil escapes
The waitress asks
if everything's OK
I tell her fine
except for the two SS officers
sitting drinking Rob Roys
pretending not to watch us
They slip a secret message
on the check
Please pay when served
Dollars or marks
I ask
She says just pay up
and spits out her gum
on the napkin
Her nametag says Barbi
I don't want to make a scene
so I pay the bill
and glance at my jr. hypnotist watch
large segments
of the world's population
have been converted by this time
saving machine
I strap to my wrist
disguised as a timex
I turn it on the SS officers
they think nothing's changed
but we know different
we know the allies
are going to bust
in here with tear gas

and submachine guns
looking for nazi jew-haters

The problem's not in the hamburgers
chili
or cokes
I explain
the problem is in being susceptible

PYGMY HEADHUNTERS AND KILLER APES,
MY LOVER AND ME *Laurel Ann Bogen*

Pygmy headhunters and killer apes play basketball at the Y. The killer apes win but the pygmy headhunters are not sore losers. They take the basketball home and boil it in your cast iron pot.

Hair. Lots of hair. Hairy devils those pygmy headhunters and killer apes. Vidal Sassoon chewed on this dilemma for awhile.

Pygmy headhunters and killer apes had flannel cakes at Musso and Franks. They were very hungry and ate three helpings each. But they wondered about the flesh beneath my flannel.

Pygmy headhunters and killer apes were homesick for Africa. They watched Make Mine Maltomeal on TV. They especially liked the part where John saved the world with gruel. It reminded everyone of home and they all had a good cry.

A cup of coffee is an honest thing. More honest than I am now. Its velocity in my veins throbs with need. I need to tell you this. You make my head hurt like sutures. You make this silly fist a killer.

Bone, hair, water, food. It is morning again. Last night the jungle used my fractured jaws to spear a message. Pygmy headhunters dance while killer apes beat their chest forget about you forget about you forget about you.

HAVANA   *Laurel Ann Bogen*

. . . .

Damp gardenias pause
this night Havana
your name a sigh
rolled on the thighs
of bronze women
Istanbul, Cairo were discarded
like petals
this is my season of Havana

Once I held a black ink pen
and wrote a word
I scarcely knew
H you emerged unsettled
a with each letter
v followed this day's vivid streets
a to find me here
n it is for you I paint my lips coral
a it is for you

Havana, you lick into corners
of the red night
drunk on Cuba Libres
and sugar cane water
tango, samba
the scratch of phonograph
beguiles the blood
to begin the tissueing off
of taffeta, corset, stockings
you move against me
your face a muzzle, a gun
a circular fan clicks seconds
"te amo" your black curls
shake and my head shakes
Yes

We rise from ashes of the night
dress and leave

we do this again and again
Havana, you are all they warned
me about: more than the sum
of my self and my others
more than that, more
you are every drug, liquor and sin
that was whispered among young girls
and still I choose you.

You take me down pungent streets
this is the street of orchids
where you wooed me
with ambiguous dilemmas
this is the street of hibiscus
where I sweep my hair away
from my face and memorize
lips tangled in strands
here are mango, indigo, papaya
slow streets that move
like sweet intoxication
until your tattoo appears
on my shoulder,
and the stretch of our bodies
pads like cats the curve
from waist to hip
the round of belly
the knowledge of muscle

Must I divulge my secrets?

This is Hard Time, Havana
a time when the wind blows black
and your name appears
on a scrap of paper on a park bench
You beckon
from the smoke stacks of Pittsburgh
and the window sills of Manchester
and are gone

I took you home
folded you away
a bureau
where your name breathes
a hot wind blowing Havana

ENGLISH FLAVORS *Laure-Anne Bosselaar*

. . . .

I love to lick English the way I licked the hard
round licorice sticks the Belgian nuns gave me for six
good conduct points on Sundays after mass.

Love it when "plethora," "indolence," "damask,"
or my new word: "lasciviousness," stain my tongue,
thicken my saliva, sweet as those sticks—black

and slick with every lick it took to make daggers
out of them: sticky spikes I brandished straight up
to the ebony crucifix in the dorm, with the pride

of a child more often punished than praised.
"Amuck," "awkward," or "knuckles," have jaw-
breaker flavors; there's honey in "hunter's moon,"

hot pepper in "hunk," and "mellifluous" has aromas
of almonds and milk. Those tastes of recompense
still bittersweet today as I roll, bend and shape

English in my mouth, repeating its syllables
like acts of contrition, then sticking out my new tongue—
flavored and sharp—to the ambiguities of meaning.

. . . .

Do you have any scissors I could borrow? *No, I'm sorry I don't.* What about a knife? You got any knives? A good paring knife would do or a simple butcher knife or maybe a cleaver? *No, sorry all I have is this old bread knife my grandfather used to butter his bread with every morning.* Well then, how about a hand drill or hammer, a bike chain, or some barbed wire? You got any rusty razor-edged barbed wire? You got a chain saw? *No, sorry I don't.* Well then maybe you might have some sticks? *I'm sorry, I don't have any sticks.* How about some stones? *No, I don't have any sticks or stones.* Well how about a stone tied to a stick? *You mean a club?* Yeah, a club. You got a club? *No, sorry, I don't have any clubs.* What about some fighting picks, war axes, military forks, or tomahawks? *No, sorry, I don't have any kind of war fork, axe, or tomahawk.* What about a morning star? *A morning star?* Yeah, you know, those spiked ball and chains they sell for riot control. *No, nothing like that. Sorry.* Now, I know you said you don't have a knife except for that dull old thing your grandfather used to butter his bread with every morning and he passed down to you but I thought maybe you just might have an Australian dagger with a quartz blade and a wood handle, or a bone dagger, or a Bowie, you know it doesn't hurt to ask? Or perhaps one of those lethal multipurpose stilettos? *No, sorry.* Or maybe you have a simple blow pipe? Or a complex airgun? *No, I don't have a simple blow pipe or a complex airgun.* Well then maybe you have a jungle carbine, a Colt, a revolver, a Ruger, an axis bolt-action repeating rifle with telescopic sight for sniping, a sawed-off shotgun? Or better yet, a gas-operated self-loading fully automatic assault weapon? *No, sorry I don't.* How about a hand grenade? *No.* How about a tank? *No.* Shrapnel? *No.* Napalm? *No.* Napalm 2. *No, sorry I don't.* Let me ask you this. Do you have any intercontinental ballistic missiles? Or submarine-launched cruise missiles? Or multiple independently targeted reentry missiles? Or terminally guided anti-tank shells or projectiles? Let me ask you this. Do you have any fission bombs or hydrogen bombs? Do you have any thermonuclear warheads? Got any electronic measures or electronic counter-measures or electronic counter-counter-measures? Got any biological weapons or germ warfare, preferably in aerosol form? Got any enhanced tactical neutron lasers emitting massive doses of whole-body gamma radiation? Wait a minute. Got any plutonium? Got any chemical agents, nerve agents, blister agents, you know, like mustard gas, any choking agents or incapacitating agents or toxin agents? *Well I'm not sure. What do they look like?* Liquid vapor powder colorless gas. Invisible. *I'm not sure. What do they smell like?* They smell like fruit, garlic, fish or soap, new-mown hay, apple blossoms, or like those little green peppers that your grandfather probably would tend to in his garden every morning after he buttered his bread with that old bread knife that he passed down to you.

DEMOGRAPHICS *Catherine Bowman*

They don't want to stop. They can't stop.
   They've been going at it for days now,
for hours, for months, for years. He's on top
   of her. She's on top of him. He's licking
her between the legs. Her fingers
   are in his mouth. It's November.
It's March. It's July and there are palms.
   Palms and humidity. It's the same man.
It's a different man. It's August and slabs
   of heat waves wallow on tarred lots.
Tornadoes sprawl across open plains.
   Temperatures rise. Rains accumulate.
Somewhere a thunderstorm dies. Somewhere
   a snow falls, colored by the red dust
of a desert. She spreads her legs. His lips
   suck her nipples. She smells his neck.
It's morning. It's night. It's noon.
   It's this year. It's last year. It's 4 A.M.
It started when the city shifted growth
   to the north, over the underground
water supply. Now the back roads are gone
   where they would drive, the deer glaring into
the headlights, Wetmore and Thousand Oaks,
   and the ranch roads that led to the hill country
and to a trio of deep moving rivers.
   There were low water crossings. Flood gauges.
Signs for falling rock. There were deer blinds
   for sale. There was cedar in the air.
Her hands are on his hips. He's pushing
   her up and down. There are so many things
she's forgotten. The names of trees. Wars.
   Recipes. The trench graves filled with hundreds.
Was it Bolivia? Argentina? Chile?
   Was it white gladioli that decorated the altar
where wedding vows were said? There was
   a dance floor. Tejano classics.
A motel. A shattered mirror. Flies.

A Sunbelt sixteen wheeler. Dairy Queens.
Gas stations. The smell of piss and cement.
   There was a field of corn, or was it cotton?
There were yellow trains and silver silos.
   They can't stop. They don't want to stop.
It's Spring, and five billion inhale
   and exhale across two hemispheres. Oceans
form currents and counter-currents.
   There was grassland. There was sugar cane.
There were oxen. Metallic ores.
   There was Timber. Fur-bearing animals.
Rice lands. Industry. Tundra. Winds
   cool the earth's surface. Thighs press
against thighs. Levels of water fluctuate.
   And yesterday a lightning bolt reached
a temperature hotter than the sun.

MONEY AS WATER *Kurt Brown*

"Cash flow" "liquid assets" "pooling our resources"—
it's clear that money falls from heaven,
drops in pennies, nickels, dimes, to gather
in the small depressions of our hands.
It's clear how profit swells and streams of money
merge, how waves of money move
through nations, cause a "rippling effect"
and soon recede. How some people
drown, while others stay afloat and keep their heads
above the flood. How banks are "bailed out"
like wounded ships and panic follows,
bubbles burst, small investors find it hard
to breathe. It's clear how money
passes through our hands like water,
and our sources, once dried up, leave us
thirsting after more. How funds
diverted, often vanish, and those without a "safety net"
go "belly up." How all we have
goes down the drain, and we get soaked.

RETURN OF THE PRODIGALS *Kurt Brown*

. . . .

*Baby boomers, the largest single generation
in history, will begin to die in great numbers
during the first decades of the 21st Century.*

How often have you made love to someone
because the Angel of Death passed by your door
throwing an icy shadow over your life—
just to let you know He's still there
in case you forgot, in case you thought
anything had changed in all these decimated centuries.

Something like that must have happened
way back then, while Hitler danced and Mussolini
grimaced for the camera. And even later,
after it was over and everyone breathed a sigh
of relief people went right on making love for awhile
and the babies kept coming and coming.

A great wave passed through the generations,
a tide of children washed up here
as if Life wanted to repopulate the world—
all those empty places at the table, all those families
shorn of parents or wiped out completely:
grandparents, aunts and uncles, even the dog.

But now it's time to call the children home.
Night's coming and shadows stretch
across the lawn as stars begin to appear
like purified souls in the blue anteroom
of evening. Death stands on tiptoe in His enormous
doorway whistling softly, as if to Himself.

And in Heaven it's quiet: a bunch of pale
Administrators chewing the fat under a single
light bulb, the moon, making them drowsy,
filling in the hollows under their eyes

so you can see they haven't slept for ages.
A little bureau somewhere on the outskirts of Time.

So no one's alarmed when the first shy spirits
appear, almost transparent in the garish
light. No one even glances up when a few more
arrive awkwardly trying out their new
wings. They're no more bothersome
than a few spectral moths hovering about the room.

But soon an almost inaudible hum
starts up, then grows louder, like the approach
of locusts or an army of men whose feet
rustle on the pavement as they march to war.
Soon the room is swarming with souls
beating wildly about in their mortal confusion.

And you are there, too, as I am,
and your brother or sister, the first girl you ever
dated, the center on your high school
football team, your best friend—
all of us somewhere in that general tumult of souls
fresh out of the story of the world.

. . . .

We librarians went to Baja last weekend and sat in the sun
Ho! Ho! It's funny, isn't it? Though not really Henry Jamesian
It's not so simple that we're prim and went to the exotic
Though perhaps that's what the story really is.
We librarians went to Baja last weekend and sat in the sun
and walked on the beach and played tennis at the Head Clerk's club
Though we were vacationing without hierarchy.
In this way I love my job, bureaucrat that I am, I love
to rank, to answer, to box; I love the Boolean in logic.
So perhaps that's why we went: Baja Mexico, if you've never been,
is about rusted cars growing into grass
on the side of the highway and shacks,
and roadside stands for olives and honey,
and Americans driving fast to the beach-and-tennis clubs they've
    built,
and the surfers in the ocean, waiting, rocking;
You see men standing in the no-man's land of the border,
waiting to cross: The border patrol jeeps with their rifles
ride by in the dust
Dirt roads and beer advertising everywhere
you look when you drive through Ensenada. We librarians
went to Baja last weekend and sat in the sun and we got a joke running:
what's the next fad in publishing after Co-Dependency?
It was a category of men who don't want to be success objects, we
    decided.
Self-help books for men who are eaten alive by women-mad-for-money.
You make them take a quiz, and everyone fits the category.
But my ex-boss, sitting there, and I are both in love with alcoholics,
She's married to hers and I've decided not to marry mine.
So maybe since we're prim and bookish we need the wild type—
I've thought about it. We laugh about these books
but just, just maybe. My ex-boss, now an administrator,
is the daughter of blacklisted Hollywood screenwriters.
She said they used to vacation right where we were when she was
    a kid.
They would dig for clams
in the bay that's going to be dredged into a marina for Americans.
Her family lived in exile, in Mexico.

She told me one day her husband doesn't believe those things
Really happened in America.
It's hard, though, to vacation without hierarchy.
Someone is the best tennis player, the best storyteller, the best
gossip, has the best body, gets along best. And you remember
where you stand as an employee. You remember
you're an American in a foreign country.
We librarians went to Baja and sat in the sun:
A day in the life, a *fête gallante*—
There was a house I wanted to run away from. Could I?

ALLEGORY OF THE SUPERMARKET *Stephanie Brown*

Procession of death,
Day-Glo death,
Potato death,
Death of strawberry.
Death strapped into a handi-six-pack
Death in vodka, scotch, the vitamin-fortified cigarette cough.
Juice of cow in a box,
Broccoli piled up man-felled trees
How long have I been in here?
Our faces look left, right, slow, so slow, so sleepy
We reach for the non-fat,
The boxes of breadsticks, the round glue of pregnancy.
No one ever says, really, anything.
Plastic bags from the roll rippp
Let's grab a lettuce from the stacks of lettuce,
Bee in the bonnet on the label of the jar of honey,
Darling: the non-world-yellow cheese,
the price,
the size chosen by a stranger's desire,
for my teeth.
Box of food for the pet at home, standing in our kitchen.
The shelves of canned fruit, yellow bullets of mustard jars
The piles of onions, the dusty garlic piles,
The triangular figure of tomatoes,
The baskets we lay our deaths down in
Fetching cans of halos.
Cry into your toilet paper,
your spray starch,
your light bulbs and lobsters in tanks near the cashier's booth
their claws held together by rubber bands
Cry into that water
Fish belly up on the Styrofoam surfaces
in refrigeration
headless feetless chickens
Turkeys across the aisle, look-alike big bodies, frozen.
Shelves of bread loaves like big leather shoes of sad old clerks
not like

smell of yeast and life's
an open wound, festering, and a feast of fools.
No dignity, my darling,
in these last three hours of the world.

He was not a kind man.
Tender would be a word he would wince at.
I think he could have had sex with any woman he desired.
He was like a man from a bodice ripper—
"Handsome, devastating."
As far as I can tell you,
He was into the seduction,
Was what they used to call a rake,
Left the women "seduced and abandoned."
You know people like this.
If you don't, you're lucky.
No one turned his head.
He sneered at women for wanting him: their foolishness was so
    embarrassing.
He could have sex by leaning the girl over a trashcan.
I didn't even think that was too weird, when I heard of it.
I knew people like this.
I knew people who routinely referred to each other as dirty words.
You know people like this.
If you don't, you're lucky.
He met a woman.
He spent the night with her.
He was ready to leave in the morning when she started to tell him
    about a book she'd read.
He'd read it; he'd never met another person who had.
They held each other, in that way of good feeling.
At that moment, his heart opened just a little bit
(—The space between the hands of the Virgin Mary, when they're
    held in front of her chest—)
Small, but big enough for a small light to shine out of.
His heart opened, and this woman happened to be there.
It could have been another woman, another place.
His time had come.
Sorry, the marriage between them didn't last.
When she left him, he felt sad, with a sadness that befits a small
    opening
With a large and benevolent protectiveness around it.

He was protected.
He couldn't endure much.
After a long time, I think he will get another chance.
Maybe another kind of love for his heart.
I'm writing his story, and I've heard
That some people, when their hearts open,
They rain stones onto the floor,
Gold coins fly like those from the jackpot of a slot machine,
A frightening and unendurable joy: I know
Some people feel their ribs widen and their bodies rack
with sobs, for how long it's taken.

HIS TOYS *Michael Dennis Browne*

We planned to keep your first toys,
preserve them; one day,
when you were grown, lead you
to a secret closet, watch you
pull wide, amazed,
re-discover your treasures.
But we can't; you're eating them.

KNOCK KNOCK *Michael Dennis Browne*

the i can't help it
is at the door
shall we admit it?
yes yes of course shrieks
the what else is new

SLEEP WALK *Christopher Buckley*

Fourteen and I knew from nothing—
but there I was in the darkened gym
to get some idea. Someone was stacking the 45s
and my friend Carlson was doing The Stroll
with Maryann Garland, gliding around the corners
of the basketball court with that strut, scuff, and easy slide.
I knew Surf Music and Motown cold, but even if
I worked up nerve to ask a girl to dance, there was no way
when it came to the Stomp, the Mash Potato,
those spins, dips, and twists kids were pulling off
like varieties of religious experience.

As recently as 8th grade, in classes the nuns
roped us into after school, I had only managed
a reluctant fox trot, as if I were dragging my shoes
through a dance floor of fudge. And those meager skills
had only led to heartbreak and Virginia Cortez,
the dark stars of her eyes burning through me
at a party where parents drank coffee in the kitchen
and came out every quarter hour to keep lights on
in the living room. She leaned her head into my shoulder
and shorted out the entire network of circuits
in my skin—and though we barely moved across
the carpet to the Statues and "Blue Velvet," sparks
stung our hands and pulled us into a world where
you could get lost in no time . . .
                              So there I was, fourteen
and through with love, putting on my best Bob Mitchum
tough-guy face, saying I'd seen it all already, and so what?
But someone switched the disks to Doo Wop, the Flamingos
and slow oldies, and the whole floor of dancers froze,
swaying only a fraction to "In the Still of the Night"
before Santo & Johnny's "Sleep Walk"
ground any pretense of movement to a halt
with its bone-deep bass laying down a line of hormones
like an infection in the blood—the high, sliding lead
seeming to lift all the sighing dreamers

out the transoms of the gym into the starlight spinning
through the blue spring night.
                                    I'd been watching a couple
in the middle—the girl, a pageboy blond, all curves
in a cotton dress, and a tall guy from the team—seniors
who'd been melting into each other all evening,
enough steam rising there to press a dozen shirts.
Both her arms hung on his neck, his arms wound around
her waist—as hot as it then got before you were thrown out
and called into the office during home room on Monday.
What wouldn't I give to be them in that dim light
and crepe paper, all confidence and careless in love?
But I knew from nothing—no one told me to be careful
what you wish for . . . And two and a half years turned me
loose in that exact spot, arms around Kathy Quigley,
eyes closed, feet stuck to the gym floor and "Sleep Walk"
stringing out a last legitimate embrace. It was time to walk out
those double metal doors, rubbing our eyes, dizzy
with our own tranced blood buzzing in the dark.
We had to kiss quickly so she could get home by 12:00—
the world still that careful and slow.
                                    I'd drive around
for an hour, up and down State, pull into Petersons for a shake,
circle the town, radio off, cruising with the windows down,
with that twang and ground swell bass from Santo & Johnny
still pulsing in my head, sure this was everything there was
despite college coming, and the war. I looked up into the night
where the stars slurred like the notes in that song
and wished again, as if I knew what I wanted . . .

the tragedy of the leaves *Charles Bukowski*

I awakened to dryness, and the ferns were dead,
the potted plants yellow as corn;
my woman was gone
and the empty bottles like bled corpses
surrounded me with their uselessness;
the sun was still good, though,
and my landlady's note cracked in fine
and undemanding yellowness, what was needed now
was a good comedian, ancient style, a jester
with jokes upon absurd pain; pain is absurd
because it exists, nothing more;
I shaved carefully with an old razor
the man who had once been young and
said to have genius; but
that's the tragedy of the leaves,
the dead ferns, the dead plants;
and I walked into a dark hall
where the landlady stood
execrating and final,
sending me to hell,
waving her fat, sweaty arms
and screaming
screaming for rent
because the world had failed us
both.

trouble with spain *Charles Bukowski*

I got in the shower
and burned my balls
last Wednesday.

met this painter called Spain,
no, he was a cartoonist,
well, I met him at a party
and everybody got mad at me
because I didn't know who he was
or what he did.

he was rather a handsome guy
and I guess he was jealous because
I was so ugly.
they told me his name
and he was leaning against the wall
looking handsome, and I said:
hey, Spain, I like that name: Spain.
but I don't like you. why don't we step out
in the garden and I'll kick the shit out of your
ass?

this made the hostess angry
and she walked over and rubbed his pecker
while I went to the crapper
and heaved.

but everybody's angry at me.
Bukowski, he can't write, he's had it,
washed up. look at him drink.
he never used to come to parties.
now he comes to parties and drinks everything
up and insults real talent.
I used to admire him when he cut his wrists
and when he tried to kill himself with
gas. look at him now leering at that 19-year-old

girl, and you know he
can't get it up.

I not only burnt my balls in that shower
last Wednesday, I spun around to get out of the burning
water, and burnt my bunghole
too.

"Gourmet kitchen" means two ovens
charred with cheese from frozen pizzas,
6 gas burners to boil water
for tea bags and instant coffee,
and a copper pot rack dangling
sauce pans stored with wedding presents,
unpacked and hung for the divorce
to jack this "custom" house's price.
"Custom" means not built of segments
hauled by semis labeled WIDE LOAD
to the building site and welded
side by side, then tied to stakes,
but, instead, framed up with presswood
sheathed in slabs of insulation
sided with strips of wood-grain vinyl,
shingled with squares of fiberglass
stapled to the "cathedral" roof.
"Cathedral" means a twenty-foot drop
from the cork fake central beam
blackened to look like Tudor oak
to the "hardwood" "great room" floor.
"Hardwood" means eighth-inch parquet tiles
glued to concrete, and the "great room,"
built on the "open plan," combines
living/dining/family "areas."
"Open" means no walls or ceilings
with costly pipes and wires inside them;
"areas" substitute for all rooms
but the bedrooms and the bathrooms—
the "half," "three-quarters" and "full" baths.
"Half" bathrooms are sinks and toilets
crammed into remodeled closets;
"three-quarter" baths have moldy showers
poorly vented by loud fans;
"full" baths feature double sinks,
his and her gold plated faucets,
built in vanities, and mirrors

framed by Hollywood marquee lights.
Bedrooms which connect to bathrooms
are called "suites" or "master suites."
"Master" means a king-sized brass bed
faces a big screen TV
to watch instead of making love.
Downstairs in the "finished" basement
("finished" means floored with outdoor carpet
and walled with knotty pine veneer)
an imitation stolen beer sign
flashes "Bud" above the wet bar
no one's ever bellied up to—
no bottle ring stains mar its counter.
Nor has any body skied
the Nordic Track or trudged the treadmill
in the basement's "exercise room"
which leads to the three car garage
with room for only one car in it.
All the other space is taken
by the "workshop's" pegboard benches
piled with oily tools and scrap
making access slightly tricky
to the sliding door's UP button.
Stand tiptoe and press it twice.
Step outside to the "private" lot,
("private" means that 8′ fencing
walls the neighbors from a yard
that's "ideal for outdoor living"—
two decks and a new croquet set!)
Interested? Then make an offer
for this contempo mini-estate.
"Priced to sell" in the mid-250s
means it won't last long at that price;
only a quarter-million dollars,
and it might be gone tomorrow.

MISS CONGENIALITY *Maxine Chernoff*

Even as an embryo, she made room for "the other guy." Slick and bloody, she emerged quietly: Why spoil the doctor's best moment? When Dad ran over her tricycle, she smiled, and when Mom drowned her kittens, she curtsied, a Swiss statuette. Her teachers liked the way she sat at her desk, composed as yesterday's news. In high school she decorated her locker with heart-shaped doilies and only went so far, a cartoon kiss at the door. She read the classics, *The Glamorous Dolly Madison*, and dreamed of marrying the boy in the choir whose voice never changed. Wedding photos reveal a waterfall where her face should be. Her husband admired how she bound her feet to buff the linoleum. When she got old, she remembered to say pardon to the children she no longer recognized, smiling sons and daughters who sat at her bedside watching her fade to a wink.

THE DEAD LETTER OFFICE *Maxine Chernoff*

Wistfulness covers the windows like drapes. Ten men armed with hankies sort the mail into two categories, letters that make them happy, letters that make them sad. Don't get me wrong. These civil servants, trusted with the awesome duty of burning millions of letters a year, do not open the envelopes like a mortician prying into the life of a client. It is the envelope itself that makes them sad. Childish handwriting scrawled to a deceased aunt makes them weep. A letter from overseas to a wife who has moved, unknown to her husband, creates such tumult that the walls quiver like jelly. Few letters are happy ones, the eviction notice never delivered, the lost bill. But when a happy letter does come into their possession, it's a red letter day. The men cheer wildly, tear up letters, and toss them out of the window, tickertape fashion. And what bliss when something intervenes and a doomed letter, like a terminally ill patient, is saved.

TOOTHACHE *Maxine Chernoff*

I never had a toothache, but the desire to have one crossed my mind constantly. Thinking a toothache was starting, I consulted a doctor who attributed the pain to a small insect bite on the left tonsil. From that day I resolved to abandon the hope of ever feeling a quick stab of pain or a steady musical throbbing. My teeth were a fortress against invaders, the health spa of an otherwise decrepit body. Sometimes I'd see people rubbing their fingers over a spot on their cheeks hot as a sidewalk in summer. Envious, I'd fall off of chairs, steps, and bicycles, trying to land on my mouth. I took up meditation and biofeedback to focus some pain in my teeth. Like children, bored with the gifts of a visiting aunt, they remained uninvolved. Finally, quite by chance I found a way to bring myself relief. Through a new medical procedure the dentist removed one healthy tooth and implanted a large decaying molar in its place. It was worth the trouble. Now, when I pass a candystore, I buy the chewiest caramels. And when I crunch on an icecube, the pain is long and complex as a medieval tapestry.

VANITY, WISCONSIN *Maxine Chernoff*

Firemen wax their mustaches at an alarm; walls with mirrors are habitually saved. At the grocery, women in line polish their shopping carts. Children too will learn that one buys meat the color of one's hair, vegetables to complement the eyes. There is no crime in Vanity, Wisconsin. Shoplifters are too proud to admit a need. Punishment, the dismemberment of a favorite snapshot, has never been practiced in modern times. The old are of no use, and once a year at their "debut," they're asked to join their reflections in Lake Lablanc. Cheerfully they dive in, vanity teaching them not to float. A visitor is not embarrassed to sparkle here or stand on his hotel balcony, taking pictures of pictures.

The first time I lied to my baby, I told him that it was his face on the baby food jar. The second time I lied to my baby, I told him that he was the best baby in the world, that I hoped he'd never leave me. Of course I want him to leave me someday. I don't want him to become one of those fat shadows who live in their mother's houses watching game shows all day. The third time I lied to my baby I said, "Isn't she nice?" of the woman who'd caressed him in his carriage. She was old and ugly and had a disease. The fourth time I lied to my baby, I told him the truth, I thought. I told him how he'd have to leave me someday or risk becoming a man in a bow tie who eats macaroni on Fridays. I told him it was for the best, but then I thought, I want him to live with me forever. Someday he'll leave me: then what will I do?

white lady *Lucille Clifton*

. . . .

a street name for cocaine

wants my son
wants my niece
wants josie's daughter
holds them hard
and close as slavery
what will it cost
to keep our children
what will it cost
to buy them back.

white lady
says i want you
whispers
let me be your lover
whispers
run me through your
fingers
feel me smell me taste me
love me
nobody understands you like
white lady

white lady
you have chained our sons
in the basement
of the big house
white lady
you have walked our daughters
out into the streets
white lady
what do we have to pay
to repossess our children
white lady
what do we have to owe
to own our own at last

wishes for sons *Lucille Clifton*

i wish them cramps.
i wish them a strange town
and the last tampon.
i wish them no 7–11.

i wish them one week early
and wearing a white skirt.
i wish them one week late.

later i wish them hot flashes
and clots like you
wouldn't believe.   let the
flashes come when they
meet someone special.
let the clots come
when they want to.

let them think they have accepted
arrogance in the universe,
then bring them to gynecologists
not unlike themselves.

I LIVE FOR MY CAR *Wanda Coleman*

can't let go of it. to live is to drive. to have it function
smooth, flawless. to rise with morning and have it start
i pray to the mechanic for heat again and air conditioning
when i meet people i used to know i'm glad to see them until
i remember what i'm driving and am afraid they'll go outside and
see me climb into that struggle buggy and laugh deep long loud

i've become very proficient at keeping my car running. i
visit service stations and repair shops often which is why
i haven't a coat to wear or nice clothes or enough money each
month to pay the rent. i don't like my car to be dirty. i spend
saturday mornings scrubbing it down. i've promised it a new
     bumper
and a paint job. luckily this year i was able to pay registration

i dream that my car is transformed into a stylish
convertible and i'm riding along happily beneath sun glasses
the desert wind kissing my face my man beside me. we smile
we are very beautiful. sometimes the dreams become nightmares
i'm careening into an intersection the kids in the back seat scream
"mama!" i mash down on the brake. the pedal goes to the floor

i have frequent fantasies about running over people i don't like
with my car.

my car's an absolute necessity in this city of cars where
you come to know people best by how they maneuver on the
     freeway
make lane changes or handle off-ramps. i've promised myself
i will one day own a luxury model. it'll be something
i can leave my children. till then i'm on spark plugs and lug nuts
keeping the one i have mobile. i live for it. can't let go of it
to drive is to live

that loosiana swamp dog put some funny stuff
on me. tells me i quiver his liver

he got the fish head eyes. smells like whiskey
pig feet and old smokes

he brings me okra and black-eyed peas
steady comes round to get his ham bone boiled

he do the belly rub
he do the jelly roll
he a back door man with front door ambition
he piss sweet water

we honky tonk we gut bucket

he scared to leave his wife she a two-headed
woman. the fix go deep

he feed me catfish promises
he feed me divorce lies

he ain't strong enuff to leave her
i ain't strong enuff to make him stay

on odd mornings he come round early
try to catch another niggah in my bed

to work his mojo he lick my pearl to
feel it glow. makes my hair grow

EMBRACE *Billy Collins*

. . . .

You know the parlor trick.
Wrap your arms around your own body
and from the back it looks like
someone is embracing you,
her hands grasping your shirt,
her fingernails teasing your neck.

From the front it is another story.
You never looked so alone,
your crossed elbows and screwy grin.
You could be waiting for a tailor
to fit you for a straitjacket,
one that would hold you really tight.

ANOTHER REASON WHY I DON'T KEEP A GUN IN THE HOUSE *Billy Collins*

The neighbors' dog will not stop barking.
He is barking the same high, rhythmic bark
that he barks every time they leave the house.
They must switch him on on their way out.

The neighbors' dog will not stop barking.
I close all the windows in the house
and put on a Beethoven symphony full blast
but I can still hear him muffled under the music,
barking, barking, barking,

and now I can see him sitting in the orchestra,
his head raised confidently as if Beethoven
had included a part for barking dog.

When the record finally ends he is still barking,
sitting there in the oboe section barking,
his eyes fixed on the conductor who is
entreating him with his baton

while the other musicians listen in respectful
silence to the famous barking dog solo,
that endless coda that first established
Beethoven as an innovative genius.

THE HISTORY TEACHER *Billy Collins*

Trying to protect his students' innocence
he told them the Ice Age was really just
the Chilly Age, a period of a million years
when everyone had to wear sweaters.

And the Stone Age became the Gravel Age,
named after the long driveways of the time.

The Spanish Inquisition was nothing more
than an outbreak of questions such as
"How far is it from here to Madrid?"
"What do you call the matador's hat?"

The War of the Roses took place in a garden,
and the Enola Gay dropped one tiny atom
on Japan.

The children would leave his classroom
for the playground to torment the weak
and the smart,
mussing up their hair and breaking their glasses,

while he gathered up his notes and walked home
past flower beds and white picket fences,
wondering if they would believe that soldiers
in the Boer War told long, rambling stories
designed to make the enemy nod off.

LITANY *Billy Collins*

. . . .

"You are the bread and the knife,
The crystal goblet and the wine . . ."
—Jacques Crickillon

You are the bread and the knife,
the crystal goblet and the wine.
You are the dew on the morning grass,
and the burning wheel of the sun.
You are the white apron of the baker
and the marsh birds suddenly in flight.

However, you are not the wind in the orchard,
the plums on the counter,
or the house of cards.
And you are certainly not the pine-scented air.
There is no way you are the pine-scented air.

It is possible that you are the fish under the bridge,
maybe even the pigeon on the general's head,
but you are not even close
to being the field of cornflowers at dusk.

And a quick look in the mirror will show
that you are neither the boots in the corner
nor the boat asleep in its boathouse.

It might interest you to know,
speaking of the plentiful imagery of the world,
that I am the sound of rain on the roof.

I also happen to be the shooting star,
the evening paper blowing down an alley,
and the basket of chestnuts on the kitchen table.

I am also the moon in the trees
and the blind woman's tea cup.
But don't worry, I am not the bread and the knife.
You are still the bread and the knife.
You will always be the bread and the knife,
not to mention the crystal goblet and—somehow—the wine.

NIGHTCLUB *Billy Collins*

You are so beautiful and I am a fool
to be in love with you
is a theme that keeps coming up
in songs and poems.
There seems to be no room for variation.
I have never heard anyone sing
I am so beautiful
and you are a fool to be in love with me,
even though this notion has surely
crossed the minds of women and men alike.
You are so beautiful, too bad you are a fool
is another one you don't hear.
Or, you are a fool to consider me beautiful.
That one you will never hear, guaranteed.

For no particular reason this afternoon
I am listening to Johnny Hartman
whose dark voice can curl around
the concepts of love, beauty, and foolishness
like no one else's can.
It feels like smoke curling up from a cigarette
someone left burning on a baby grand piano
around three o'clock in the morning;
smoke that billows up into the bright lights
while out there in the darkness
some of the beautiful fools have gathered
around little tables to listen,
some with their eyes closed,
others leaning forward into the music
as if it were holding them up,
or twirling the loose ice in a glass,
slipping by degrees into a rhythmic dream.

Yes, there is all this foolish beauty,
borne beyond midnight,
that has no desire to go home,
especially now when everyone in the room
is watching the large man with the tenor sax

that hangs from his neck like a golden fish.
He moves forward to the edge of the stage
and hands the instrument down to me
and nods that I should play.
So I put the mouthpiece to my lips
and blow into it with all my living breath.
We are all so foolish,
my long bebop solo begins by saying,
so damn foolish
we have become beautiful without even knowing it.

THINGS MY GRANDFATHER MUST HAVE SAID *Mark Cox*

I want to die in the wintertime,
make the ground regret it,
make the backhoe sweat.

January. Blue Monday
after the holiday weekend.
I want it to be hard on everybody.

I want everyone to have a headache
and the traffic to be impossible.
Back it up for miles, Jesus.

I want steam under the hood, bad directions,
cousins lost, babies crying, and sleet.
I want a wind so heavy their umbrellas howl.

And give me some birds, pigeons even,
anything circling for at least half an hour,
and plastic tulips and a preacher who stutters

"Uh" before every word of Psalm 22.
I want to remind them just how bad things are.
Spell my name wrong on the stone, import

earthworms fat as Aunt Katie's arms
and put them under the folding chairs.
And I want a glass coffin,

I want to be wearing the State of Missouri
string tie that no one else liked . . . God,
I hope the straps break

and I fall in with a thud. I hope
the shovel slips out of my son's hands.
I want them to remember I don't feel anything.

I want the food served straight from my garden.
I want the head of the table set. I want
everyone to get a pennant that says,

"Gramps was the greatest,"
and a complete record of my mortgage payments
in every thank-you note.

And I want to keep receiving mail for thirteen years,
all the bills addressed to me,
old friends calling every other month

to wonder how I am.
Then I want an earthquake or rising water-table,
the painful exhumation of my remains.

I want to do it all again.

I want to die the day before something truly
important happens and have my grandson say:
What would he have thought of that.

I want you all to know how much I loved you.

THE GARGLERS *Mark Cox*

The sun rises on a professor gargling. Because it is morning,
gargling makes perfect sense to him. Overnight
a great drama has taken place in his mouth—growth,
decay, procreation—the whole gambit, schmear, shebang.
As he gargles, he hums his morning fight song
which helps him disregard the mob with torches in his mouth.
I have my health, he hums, and you can't take that away from me.
He consults his watch—almost two minutes now, nothing
can have survived above the gumline, surely by now
he more or less has his mouth to himself.
In fact, the lining of his mouth itself
has begun to question his jurisdiction over it.
A terrific stillness has fallen over the bathroom,
as if the sink and every pipe are waiting for him to spit.
He's just approaching a particularly crucial octave change
when his wife leans in and asks, "do you love me?"
He nods, pointing to his watch, but with a look that says,
"You know how important fresh breath is to rhetoricians."
"If you really loved me," her look says, "you'd say so.
You'd splatter whatever was keeping you from telling me
all over yourself in order to keep me."
He looks from his underarm spray to his cologne and back again.
It is morning. Gargling makes perfect sense. But he expectorates
and says, "I love you, do you love me too?"
But it's too late, because his wife already has a mouthful
and is gargling and pointing at her mouth as if to say,
how could you ever doubt it . . .

Today, a coed with a black eye
and bruised cheek stopped me
in the hall to ask, anxiously,
where does one put "Jr."
according to standard manuals
on style?

"In jail?" I said. "No, really," she said,
"This is important."

FORM REJECTION LETTER *Philip Dacey*

We are sorry we cannot use the enclosed.
We are returning it to you.
We do not mean to imply anything by this.
We would prefer not to be pinned down about this matter.
But we are not keeping—cannot, will not keep—
  what you sent us.
We did receive it, though, and our returning it to you
   is a sign of that.
It was not that we minded your sending it to us
   unasked.
That is happening all the time, they
   come when we least expect them,
   when we forget we have needed or might yet need them,
   and we send them back.
We send this back.
It is not that we minded.
At another time, there is no telling . . .
But this time, it does not suit our present needs.

We wish to make it clear it was not easy receiving it.
It came so encumbered.
And we are busy here.
We did not feel
   we could take it on.
We know it would not have ended there.
It would have led to this, and that.
We know about these things.
It is why we are here.
We wait for it. We recognize it when it comes.
Regretfully, this form letter does not allow us to elaborate
   why we sent it back.
It is not that we minded.

We hope this does not discourage you. But we would not
   want to encourage you falsely.
It requires delicate handling, at this end.
If we had offered it to you,
   perhaps you would understand.

But, of course, we did not.
You cannot know what your offering it meant to us,
And we cannot tell you:
There is a form we must adhere to.
It is better for everyone that we use this form.

As to what you do in future,
    we hope we have given you signs,
    that you have read them,
    that you have not mis-read them.
We wish we could be more helpful.
But we are busy.
We are busy returning so much.
We cannot keep it.
It all comes so encumbered.
And there is no one here to help.
Our enterprise is a small one.
We are thinking of expanding.
We hope you will send something.

COKE *Philip Dacey*

I was proud of the Coca-Cola stitched in red
on the pocket of my dad's shirt,
just above his heart.
Coca-Cola was America
and my dad drove its truck.

I loved the way the letters curved,
like handwriting, something personal,
a friendly offer of a drink
to a man in need. Bring me your poor,
your thirsty.

And on every road I went, faces
under the sign of Coke smiled down
out of billboards at me. We were all
brothers and sisters in the family
of man, our bottles to our lips,
tipping our heads back to the sun.

My dad lifted me up when he came home,
his arms strong from stacking
case after case of Coke all day. A couple of
cold ones always waited for us in the kitchen.

I believed our President and my dad
were partners. My dad said someday Coke
would be sold in every country in the world,
and when that happened there would be
no more wars. "Who can imagine," he asked,
"two people fighting while they swig their Cokes?"
I couldn't. And each night before sleep,
I thanked God for my favorite drink.

When I did, I imagined him tilting the bottle
up to his heavenly lips, a little Coke
dribbling down his great white beard.

And sometimes I even thought of his
son on the cross, getting vinegar
but wanting Coke. I knew that if I
had been there, I would have handed a Coke
up to him, who would have figured out
how to take it, even though his hands
were nailed down good, because he was God.
And I would have said when he took it,
"That's from America, Jesus. I hope
you like it." And then I'd have watched,
amidst the thunder and lightning
on that terrible hill, Jesus' Adam's apple
bob up and down as he drained that bottle
in one long divine swallow
like a sweaty player at a sandlot game
between innings, the crucial ninth
coming up next.

And then the dark, sweet flood
of American sleep,
sticky and full of tiny bubbles,
would pour over me.

SQUEAK *Philip Dacey*

. . . .

"Let's do it quietly, my mom and dad aren't asleep yet."
— She to him

Let the springs squeak.
Let the whole world
hear the springs squeak.
Let that squeaking
be the new
music of the heavenly spheres.
Let no one oil
the squeaking springs.
Let all springs always
everywhere
be rusty or tight
and squeak, squeak.
Let anyone under
this roof
who hears a squeak
and can't stand it
live
on top of the roof.
Let the weather
teach that lover
of quiet
how to squeak.

Let the silence
when the squeaking springs
stop
be
like the first
eclipse
to the first
man or woman on earth.
Let the only acceptable response
to one squeak be
another.
And let the night

be filled
with a chorus of squeaks
like the anthem of frogs
in a pond, fat,
up to their necks in muck,
and happy to be there
as the stars squeak
their way across the sky.

THE RULES *Philip Dacey*

*"Women is not allow in you room; if you burn you bed
you going out; only on Sunday you can sleep all day."*
— *Sign in Pioneer Inn, Maui, Hawaii*

Keep you trouble to youself.
We no want more than that
We got. We call police if
You money is hot.

If you lonely, go on street
Make good time.
No sit in room for weep
And call her name.

If feel good, keep down
You singing. We got all
Work to do, no time
For happy fooling.

You pay before you sleep.
You no sleep, we keep
You money. If
Don't you like, is tough.

When hot go cold
The water, blow on it
Or do without. Be glad
You got what you got.

Follow rules
Or we go bust you head.
In room no sales
And keep you shoes off bed.

THE HOAGIE SCAM *Jim Daniels*

Two kids in baggy jeans
at the door selling hoagies
for the church.

*They're putting something bad
in the water*, one kid says.
Church wants to stop it.

Makes us a little crazy
the other kid says. Their eyeballs
are moons wide open

to all things
dark. In other words,
blind on smoked rocks.

*Yeah, we got some good
hoagies. Pure hoagies.*
They're laughing at each

other like I'm not even
there, holding the door open
to November cold, my wife

and kid dropping pots
and pans behind me in the kitchen
as I firmly pull the door

toward me. *Hey man, buy our hoagies
we need to sell lots of hoagies.*
Back on track, the other chimes in,

For our church. For new uniforms.
They look 17 plus 5 for bad
behavior. One kid grabs the door.

He's in my face. I give them
each a dollar. *That's half
a hoagie*, one says, *only half,*

but I guess that's good enough
for now. I'm mad enough
to ask about delivery.

They're mad enough to write
down my order on a scrap of paper.
It's for a good cause, they both say.

I liked the girls and the chocolate
pretzels better, more subtle, almost
believable. Why do I even answer

the door? The neighbors don't.
I stand in the grey fog of dusk
and watch them walk away.

I try not to be afraid or foolish
crunching over the rubble of city
streets. My child in the kitchen

is growing up here. I'll have to tell
him something about God soon.
And hoagie salesmen from the moon

and lost hearts fluttering away
and lost hopes stumbling over
city bridges. *I'm trying to put*

a few leaves back on the trees,
I tell my wife. *We need those leaves,*
she says. I make my own hoagie

for a late-night snack,
just to remember what one tastes like.
I slather on the mustard. Outside,

my porch light burns bright.

BLESSING THE HOUSE *Jim Daniels*

I step out of the car and stare
at the flat houses with their bristly bushes
wild and short like my old hair.
I want to cut my hair and spread it over this snowy yard
like my own ashes, I want to curl inside a sidewalk square
my ear to the ground, cupped, listening—what could I bring
back to life? Would I hear the rough chalk scrawl over cement?

This house the priest blessed over thirty years ago
when the lawn was mud and boards. *Bless this house,*
I think, standing in the street. The wind blows cold
but I know this wind, its harsh front.
Don't try to bully me, I say. I am home
and my hands are trembling, I am sighing.
The car door slams. I clap my hands
for the hell of it, a clap on a street corner
echoing a little, among friends.

Once I stood here for hours
trying to hit the streetlight with a snowball,
to leave a white smudge. I have left no smudge,
nothing I could call mine. The grey sky presses
down on these small houses, on my parents' house
and its square slab. They are inside,
maybe changing the channel on the TV, maybe
grabbing a beer and a bowl of chips, maybe
flushing the toilet, maybe scrubbing their faces,
maybe peering out a dark window.

I am waiting to step inside for the hug and the kiss,
I am waiting to push away this grey sadness—cement and sky.
I grab a handful of snow and touch it to my forehead
where it melts down my face. I smudge my chest
with an X of snow, I toss handfuls on the yard,
on the scraped sidewalk—ashes, ashes, glowing
in the streetlight before the melting, the disappearing.

Oh glorious snow, I say, *we have missed each other.*
I listen for a moment. I lift my bags from the trunk.
The porch light glows its yellow basket
of tender light. I stomp my boots, and I go in.

PONY EXPRESS *Stephen Dobyns*

—For Mary Karr

Some would have you think the Pony Express
is dead. Don't believe it. They're only waiting.
You know the letter you thought of writing
to that woman you once loved, the one describing
how you remembered her hair or hands or
the curve of her chin? That's the sort of letter
they now deal in, and if you wrote it,
they would show up to take it. These days
the riders like apologies, regrets, the letters
that begin: If only I had known then
what I know now—these aged men with their
aged ponies, playing cards and polishing
their saddles in the city's only livery stable,
waiting for someone's change of heart.
Take the example of the old clerk who lives
by himself in a cheap room. Forty years ago
he loved a woman and now he dreams of her face.
If only he wrote, Sometimes, I think of you;
sometimes, I still desire you; sometimes,
I wish I could hear you laugh once again.
Then suddenly there would appear at the door
a frail old man in a cowboy hat and gunfighter
mustache. He'd take that letter and, oh,
he would ride. He'd gallop his pony across
highways, expressways, railways, even
airport runways until at last he reached
the cottage of a bright-cheeked old woman
who would read the letter with one hand pressed
to her heart as the sunset twinkled and
from somewhere came the twittering of violins.
But of course the old clerk won't write the letter,
and as the world gets colder, he gets smaller;
and as the world gets harder, he gets meaner.
At night he perches over his hot plate
watching the sun collapse behind the high rises,

while across the city a last Pony Express rider
sticks his head from the stable door to see what
final shenanigans the setting sun is up to.
Why is it, they both think, that some days the sun
just seems to flash out as if someone had snatched
up its last light and smashed it to the ground?

CONFESSION *Stephen Dobyns*

. . . .

The Nazi within me thinks it's time to take charge.
The world's a mess; people are crazy.
The Nazi within me wants windows shut tight,
new locks put on the doors. There's too much
fresh air, too much coming and going.
The Nazi within me wants more respect. He wants
the only TV camera, the only bank account,
the only really pretty girl. The Nazi within me
wants to be boss of traffic and traffic lights.
People drive too fast; they take up too much space.
The Nazi within me thinks people are getting away
with murder. He wants to be boss of murder.
He wants to be boss of bananas, boss of white bread.
The Nazi within me wants uniforms for everyone.
He wants them to wash their hands, sit up straight,
pay strict attention. He wants to make certain
they say yes when he says yes, no when he says no.
He imagines everybody sitting in straight chairs,
people all over the world sitting in straight chairs.
Are you ready? he asks them. They say they are ready.
Are you ready to be happy? he asks them. They say
they are ready to be happy. The Nazi within me wants
everyone to be happy but not too happy and definitely
not noisy. No singing, no dancing, no carrying on.

HOW TO LIKE IT *Stephen Dobyns*

These are the first days of fall. The wind
at evening smells of roads still to be traveled,
while the sound of leaves blowing across the lawns
is like an unsettled feeling in the blood,
the desire to get in a car and just keep driving.
A man and a dog descend their front steps.
The dog says, Let's go downtown and get crazy drunk.
Let's tip over all the trash cans we can find.
This is how dogs deal with the prospect of change.
But in his sense of the season, the man is struck
by the oppressiveness of his past, how his memories
which were shifting and fluid have grown more solid
until it seems he can see remembered faces
caught up among the dark places in the trees.
The dog says, Let's pick up some girls and just
rip off their clothes. Let's dig holes everywhere.
Above his house, the man notices wisps of cloud
crossing the face of the moon. Like in a movie,
he says to himself, a movie about a person
leaving on a journey. He looks down the street
to the hills outside of town and finds the cut
where the road heads north. He thinks of driving
on that road and the dusty smell of the car
heater, which hasn't been used since last winter.
The dog says, Let's go down to the diner and sniff
people's legs. Let's stuff ourselves on burgers.
In the man's mind, the road is empty and dark.
Pine trees press down to the edge of the shoulder,
where the eyes of animals, fixed in his headlights,
shine like small cautions against the night.
Sometimes a passing truck makes his whole car shake.
The dog says, Let's go to sleep. Let's lie down
by the fire and put our tails over our noses.
But the man wants to drive all night, crossing
one state line after another, and never stop
until the sun creeps into his rearview mirror.
Then he'll pull over and rest awhile before
starting again, and at dusk he'll crest a hill

and there, filling a valley, will be the lights
of a city entirely new to him.
But the dog says, Let's just go back inside.
Let's not do anything tonight. So they
walk back up the sidewalk to the front steps.
How is it possible to want so many things
and still want nothing? The man wants to sleep
and wants to hit his head again and again
against a wall. Why is it all so difficult?
But the dog says, Let's go make a sandwich.
Let's make the tallest sandwich anyone's ever seen.
And that's what they do and that's where the man's
wife finds him, staring into the refrigerator
as if into the place where the answers are kept—
the ones telling why you get up in the morning
and how it is possible to sleep at night,
answers to what comes next and how to like it.

EGO *Denise Duhamel*

I just didn't get it—
even with the teacher holding an orange (the earth) in one hand
and a lemon (the moon) in the other,
her favorite student (the sun) standing behind her with a flashlight.
I just couldn't grasp it—
this whole citrus universe, these bumpy planets revolving so slowly
no one could even see themselves moving.
I used to think if I could only concentrate hard enough
I could be the one person to feel what no one else could,
sense a small tug from the ground, a sky shift, the earth changing
    gears.
Even though I was only one mini-speck on a speck,
even though I was merely a pinprick in one goosebump on the
    orange,
I was sure then I was the most specially perceptive, perceptively
    sensitive.
I was sure then my mother was the only mother to snap,
"The world doesn't revolve around you!"
The earth was fragile and mostly water,
just the way the orange was mostly water if you peeled it,
just the way I was mostly water if you peeled me.
Looking back on that third grade science demonstration,
I can understand why some people gave up on fame or religion or
    cures—
especially people who have an understanding
of the excruciating crawl of the world,
who have a well-developed sense of spatial reasoning
and the tininess that it is to be one of us.
But not me—even now I wouldn't mind being god, the force
who spins the planets the way I spin a globe, a basketball, a yoyo.
I wouldn't mind being that teacher who chooses the fruit,
or that favorite kid who gives the moon its glow.

I'M DEALING WITH MY PAIN *Denise Duhamel*

He's about 300 pounds and knows martial arts, boxing and wrestling—both the real and the fake kind. So I never know when I'm thrown to the ground or hurled against the ropes of a boxing ring fence (who can guess when he'll surprise me with a punch next?) if the ache in my back is real or cartoon, if my bruises will stay or wash off like kiddie tattoos.

Pain is a sneak and a cheat. He loves to eat unhealthy foods (scrapple, greasy gravy, Little Debbie Snacks). Not only that—I think he smokes. I can smell it on his breath, all fire and ash, when he pins me to my bed without asking. He's hefty and invisible and likes to strike in the dark so that even my magnifying glass and double locks are useless. Sometimes I call him Sumo, the Devil, or any member of my family. He's a changeling and a scam. His footprints are the ones that make cracks in the sidewalk.

Pain first introduced himself as a sadist. I was confused at the time. He said he was seduced by the blue of my wrist, the soft hollow at the center of my throat. He squeezed my heart like a Nerf ball until it was all lumps and fingernail marks. I nursed Pain like a mother. I tried to cheer him up like a sister, but everyone knows how that story goes.

Pain and I did have a few good times, if you can call them that. Eating ice cream under the covers, our tears drying on our cheeks so they chapped. We liked to go to movies alone. Pain, being invisible, snuck in without paying, then he'd leave the seat next to mine and feel up another girl in the theater. I could always tell which one. I'd hear her crying the way I did or crunching her popcorn as though each kernel was a small bone in Pain's neck or foot. He still comes around, though I tell him it's over, though I spit into his round hairy face.

He just laughs that sexy laugh. You know, the kind that gets in your head and you can't tell if it's making you nauseous or turning you on. There's no restraining order that works on Pain, the outlaw who loves to chase and embrace us, the outlaw we sometimes love to chase and embrace.

WHY, ON A BAD DAY, I CAN RELATE
TO THE MANATEE *Denise Duhamel*

The manatee tries a diet of only sea grass, but still stays fat.
Mistaking her for a mermaid from afar,
sailors of long ago lost interest when they got too close,
openly making fun of her chubbiness. She knows Rodney
    Dangerfield
would write jokes about her if she were more popular.
She's ashamed of her crooked teeth, her two big molars
that leave her sucking and grinding
with bad table manners. She swims towards danger
over and over, scars from motor boats on her back
reminders of her slow stupidness. She resents being called
a sea-cow. She hopes her whiskers don't show
in the light. She is the mammal who knows
about low self-esteem. I first met her on my honeymoon
in southern Florida. I was on a cruise in my one piece bathing suit.
The women in bikinis squealed and pointed to the nearby dolphins,
clapping so their sleek gray backs would come to the water's surface.
In the shadow of her prettier ocean sister, the manatee swam by
    also.
No one but I paid her much attention. I wanted to lend her
my make-up, massage her spine, lend a girl-friend-ear
and listen to her underwater troubles. I dreamt of her
as I slept in the warmth of my new husband. I dreamt of her
as he slept in the warmth of me. On a good day, too,
I can relate to the manatee, who knows
on some level that she is endangered
and believes in mating for life.

BUDDHIST BARBIE *Denise Duhamel*

· ·

—For Nick

In the 5th century B.C.
an Indian philosopher Gautama
teaches "All is emptiness"
and "There is no self."
In the 20th century A.D.
Barbie agrees, but wonders how a man
with such a belly could pose,
smiling, and without a shirt.

ON HEARING THE AIRLINES WILL USE A PSYCHOLOGICAL PROFILE TO CATCH POTENTIAL SKYJACKERS *Stephen Dunn*

. . . .

They will catch me
as sure as the check-out girls
in every Woolworths have caught me, the badge
of my imagined theft shining in their eyes.

I will be approaching the ticket counter
and knowing myself, myselves,
will effect the nonchalance of a baron.
That is what they'll be looking for.

I'll say "Certainly is nice that the
airlines are taking these precautions,"
and the man behind the counter
will press a secret button;

there'll be a hand on my shoulder
(this will have happened before in a dream),
and in a back room they'll ask me
"Why were you going to do it?"

I'll say "You wouldn't believe
I just wanted to get to Cleveland?"
"No," they'll say.
So I'll tell them everything,

the plot to get the Pulitzer Prize
in exchange for the airplane,
the bomb in my pencil,
heroin in the heel of my boot.

Inevitably, it'll be downtown for booking,
newsmen pumping me for deprivation
during childhood,
the essential cause.

"There is no one cause for any human act,"
I'll tell them, thinking finally,
a chance to let the public in
on the themes of great literature.

And on and on, celebrating myself, offering
no resistance, assuming what they assume,
knowing, in a sense, there is no such thing
as the wrong man.

AT THE SMITHVILLE METHODIST CHURCH *Stephen Dunn*

It was supposed to be Arts & Crafts for a week,
but when she came home
with the "Jesus Saves" button, we knew what art
was up, what ancient craft.

She liked her little friends. She liked the songs
they sang when they weren't
twisting and folding paper into dolls.
What could be so bad?

Jesus had been a good man, and putting faith
in good men was what
we had to do to stay this side of cynicism,
that other sadness.

O.K., we said. One week. But when she came home
singing "Jesus loves me,
the Bible tells me so," it was time to talk.
Could we say Jesus

doesn't love you? Could I tell her the Bible
is a great book certain people use
to make you feel bad? We sent her back
without a word.

It had been so long since we believed, so long
since we needed Jesus
as our nemesis and friend, that we thought he was
sufficiently dead,

that our children would think of him like Lincoln
or Thomas Jefferson.
Soon it became clear to us: you can't teach disbelief
to a child,

only wonderful stories, and we hadn't a story
nearly as good.
On parents' night there were the Arts & Crafts
all spread out

like appetizers. Then we took our seats
in the church
and the children sang a song about the Ark,
and Hallelujah

and one in which they had to jump up and down
for Jesus.
I can't remember ever feeling so uncertain
about what's comic, what's serious.

Evolution is magical but devoid of heroes.
You can't say to your child
"Evolution loves you." The story stinks
of extinction and nothing

exciting happens for centuries. I didn't have
a wonderful story for my child
and she was beaming. All the way home in the car
she sang the songs,

occasionally standing up for Jesus.
There was nothing to do
but drive, ride it out, sing along
in silence.

THE SHAME PLACE *Stephen Dunn*

After he did what he did, and was ashamed,
   he went into himself
where shame makes its poor home

and lived there amid the excessive heat,
   the Dead End signs.
Shame was his rent and he paid in shame

until it was spent and he returned
   to his public body
which was waiting like a debtor

to apologize. He never felt so clean.
   At work,
where it was expensive to be ashamed,

he wished everyone could visit
   their shame place,
could live for a while without credit

or esteem. He felt sorry for everyone
   unchanged.
But there was no hope for the shameless

with their profit charts and perfect reasons.
   And what could he say
to the beaten who had lived too long

eating their hearts and words?
   Their shame places
were hovels, all the energy shut off.

Soon he lied again, hurt someone, rekindled
   what never burns to ash.
Once again his shame place opened and took

him in. It had carpets. A plush chair
   covered the spot
where he had sat and writhed.

THE RETIREMENT OF THE ELEPHANT *Russell Edson*

An elephant of long service to a circus retired to a small cottage on a quiet street, to spend its remaining days in the study of life after death.

It had looked forward to these quiet years, when the mind would be readied for the coming collapse of the biology.

But the elephant found that it was too big to fit through the front door. The elephant pushed through anyway, smashing the front of the cottage. As it started upstairs to the bathroom it fell into the cellar.

The elephant climbed out and went to the back of the cottage and broke in again, pushing down the remaining walls.

Now the elephant realizes that its only course is to run amuck— Yes, just to run amuck!

Goddamn everything!

THE AUTOMOBILE *Russell Edson*

....

A man had just married an automobile.

But I mean to say, said his father, that the automobile is not a person because it is something different.

For instance, compare it to your mother. Do you see how it is different from your mother? Somehow it seems wider, doesn't it? And besides, your mother wears her hair differently.

You ought to try to find something in the world that looks like mother.

I have mother, isn't that enough of a thing that looks like mother? Do I have to gather more mothers?

They are all old ladies who do not in the least excite any wish to procreate, said the son.

But you cannot procreate with an automobile, said father.

The son shows father an ignition key. See, here is a special penis which does with the automobile as the man with the woman; and the automobile gives birth to a place far from this place, dropping its puppy miles as it goes.

Does that make me a grandfather? said father.

That makes you where you are when I am far away, said the son.

Father and mother watch an automobile with a just married sign on it growing smaller in a road.

COUNTING SHEEP *Russell Edson*

....

A scientist has a test tube full of sheep. He wonders if he should try to shrink a pasture for them.

They are like grains of rice.

He wonders if it is possible to shrink something out of existence.

He wonders if the sheep are aware of their tininess, if they have any sense of scale. Perhaps they just think the test tube is a glass barn ...

He wonders what he should do with them; they certainly have less meat and wool than ordinary sheep. Has he reduced their commercial value?

He wonders if they could be used as a substitute for rice, a sort of woolly rice ...

He wonders if he just shouldn't rub them into a red paste between his fingers.

He wonders if they're breeding, or if any of them have died.

He puts them under a microscope and falls asleep counting them ...

THE CATEGORIES *Russell Edson*

....

A man wants an aeroplane to like him. He doesn't like it, but he wants it to like him. The aeroplane doesn't.

He says, like me.

The aeroplane doesn't; and likes him even less than it might have, had he not pushed himself on it.

Like me, screams the man, you rotten king of the poopers!

The aeroplane considers him one of those mentally defective things that constantly go outside their category to find other things to like them because theirs doesn't.

Well, I don't like you neither, you kinky thingumajig! You snotty despicable! You rum-crazy dummy! You shit-faced carrot! You applesauced whacker! You collie dog without a nose! You sugarplummed dowager!

Meanwhile, the aeroplane has fallen asleep.

The man screams, wake up, you carpet tack! You ticklish custard. Wake up, you clever sap, and like me, because my category doesn't ...

87

GOOD SON JIM *Russell Edson*

Poor people who do not have the price of a fence ask son Jim to be a fence for the chicken yard, that is, until their ship comes in; which no one believes because they live inland.

But what's the good of a fence around a chicken yard where there ain't no chickens?

Did you eat them chickens, Jim?

No, we ain't never had no chickens.

Then what are you doing fencing what we ain't got?

I don't know, I forget . . .

Maybe you better be a chicken. But don't wander away, because we ain't got a fence to keep that stupid bird from wandering into the neighbor's yard and getting itself killed for Sunday dinner, said his father.

Heck, I'll just peck around the house; lots of tasty worms under the porch, said son Jim.

APE *Russell Edson*

You haven't finished your ape, said mother to father, who had monkey hair and blood on his whiskers.

I've had enough monkey, cried father.

You didn't eat the hands, and I went to all the trouble to make onion rings for its fingers, said mother.

I'll just nibble on its forehead, and then I've had enough, said father.

I stuffed its nose with garlic, just like you like it, said mother.

Why don't you have the butcher cut these apes up? You lay the whole thing on the table every night; the same fractured skull, the same singed fur; like someone who died horribly. These aren't dinners, these are post-mortem dissections.

Try a piece of its gum, I've stuffed its mouth with bread, said mother.

Ugh, it looks like a mouth full of vomit. How can I bite into its cheek with bread spilling out of its mouth? cried father. Break one of the ears off, they're so crispy, said mother.

I wish to hell you'd put underpants on these apes; even a jockstrap, screamed father.

Father, how dare you insinuate that I see the ape as anything more than simple meat, screamed mother.

Well, what's with this ribbon tied in a bow on its privates? screamed father.

Are you saying that I am in love with this vicious creature? That I would submit my female opening to this brute? That after we had love on the kitchen floor I would put him in the oven, after breaking his head with a frying pan; and then serve him to my husband, that my husband might eat the evidence of my infidelity . . . ?

I'm just saying that I'm damn sick of ape every night, cried father.

ELEPHANT TEARS *Russell Edson*

. . . .

An elephant asked another elephant if its tusks were mustaches, or just unkempt nose hair.

Nose hair? said the second elephant.

Those big things sticking out of where your nostrils would start, if they started.

Nostrils?

I don't know, someplace under that big nose, said the first elephant.

What big nose? said the second elephant.

That thing hanging out of your face like a fifth leg.

What thing? said the second elephant, searching its face with its trunk.

That thing hanging over your defeated mouth, which incidentally, is certainly nothing to write home about.

But why would you want to write home about my mouth? said the second elephant.

Wait, I know what's wrong with you, your whole head's been taken over by your nose. You're just one big nose; a nasal monster!

Oh, no, how could that have happened? wept the second elephant, wiping its elephant tears with its trunk . . .

THE CRUMBLE-KNEES *Russell Edson*

. . . .

There was once a man who went down on his knee to ask a woman to marry him. But just as he would make the question his knee crumbled.

The woman's father, who had been listening behind a curtain, stepped out and said, get out of here, you Crumble-Knee.

No no, cried the man, my other knee is fine; if you'll just give me another chance I'll go right down on it.

Well, all right, said the father, but I'm going to hide behind this curtain just to make sure.

And so the man went down on his other knee. But just as he would make the question his knee crumbled.

That's it, cried the father, rushing out from behind the curtain, get out of here, you Crumble-Knees!

And so the man dragged himself to his mother's house.
She asked what happened.
My knees crumbled just as I would ask a woman to be my wife.
But you're not ready for marriage, she said.
It was my knees, mom, they just wouldn't take it.
Of course not, she said, and just think of the coitus.

And so the man dragged himself down into the cellar of his mother's house. And there in the darkness began to think of the coitus . . .

THE WHITE DRESS *Lynn Emanuel*

What does it feel like to be this shroud
on a hanger, this storm cloud hanging
in the closet? We itch to feel it, it itches
to be felt, it feels like an itch—

encrusted with beading, it's an eczema
of sequins, rough, gullied, riven,
puckered with stitchery, a frosted window
against which we long to put our tongues,

a vase for holding the long-stemmed
bouquet of a woman's body.
Or it's armor and it fits like a glove.
The buttons run like rivets down the front.

When we're in it we're machinery,
a cutter nosing the ocean of a town.
Right now it's lonely locked up
in the closet; while we're busy

fussing at our vanity, it hangs there
in the drooping waterfall of itself,
a road with no one on it, bathed
in moonlight, rehearsing its lines.

THE POLITICS OF NARRATIVE:
WHY I AM A POET *Lynn Emanuel*

. . . .

Jill's a good kid who's had some tough luck. But that's another story. It's a day when the smell of fish from Tib's hash house is so strong you could build a garage on it. We are sitting in Izzy's where Carl has just built us a couple of solid highballs. He's okay, Carl is, if you don't count his Roamin' Hands and Rushin' Fingers. Then again, that should be the only trouble we have in this life. Anyway, Jill says, "Why don't you tell about It? Nobody ever gets the poet's point of view." I don't know, maybe she's right. Jill's just a kid, but she's been around; she knows what's what.

So, I tell Jill, we are at Izzy's just like now when he comes in. And the first thing I notice is his hair, which has been Vitalis-ed into sub- mission. But, honey, it won't work, and it gives him a kind of rumpled your-boudoir-or-mine look. I don't know why I noticed that before I noticed his face. Maybe it was just the highballs doing the looking. Anyway, then I see his face, and I'm telling you—I'm telling Jill—this is a masterpiece of a face.

But—and this is the god's own truth—I'm tired of beauty. Really. I know, given all that happened, this must sound kind of funny, but it made me tired just to look at him. That's how beautiful he was, and how much he spelled T-R-O-U-B-L-E. So I threw him back. I mean, I didn't say it, I say to Jill, with my mouth. But I said it with my eyes and my shoulders. I said it with my heart. I said, Honey, I'm throwing you back. And looking back, that was the worst, I mean, the worst thing— bar none—that I could have done, because it drew him like horseshit draws flies. I mean, he didn't walk over and say, "Hello, girls; hey, you with the dark hair, your indifference draws me like horseshit draws flies."

But he said it with his eyes. And then he smiled. And that smile was a gas station on a dark night. And as wearying as all the rest of it. I am many things, but dumb isn't one of them. And here is where I say to Jill, "I just can't go on." I mean, how we get from the smile into the bedroom, how it all happens, and what all happens, just bores me. I am a conceptual storyteller. In fact, I'm a conceptual liver. I prefer the cookbook to the actual meal. Feeling bores me. That's why I write poetry. In poetry you just give the instructions to the reader and say, "Reader, you go on from here." And what I like about poetry is its readers, because those are giving people. I mean, those are people you can trust to get the job done. They pull their own weight. If I had to have someone at my back in a dark alley, I'd want it to be a poetry reader. They're not like some people, who maybe do it right if you tell them, "Put this foot down, and now put that one in front of the other, button your coat, wipe your nose."

So, really, I do it for the readers who work hard and, I feel, deserve something better than they're used to getting. I do it for the working stiff. And I write for people, like myself, who are just tired of the trickle-down theory where somebody spends pages and pages on some fat book where everything including the draperies, which happen to be *burnt orange*, are described, and, further, are some *metaphor* for something. And this whole boggy waste trickles down to the reader in the form of a little burp of feeling. God, I hate prose. I think the average reader likes ideas.

"A sentence, unlike a line, is not a station of the cross." I said this to the poet Mark Strand. I said, "I could not stand to write prose; I could not stand to have to write things like 'the draperies were burnt orange and the carpet was brown.'" And he said, "You could do it if that's all you did, if that was the beginning and the end of your novel." So please, don't ask me for a little trail of bread crumbs to get from the smile to the bedroom, and from the bedroom to the death at the end, although you can ask me a lot about death. That's all I like, the very beginning and the very end. I haven't got the stomach for the rest of it.

I don't think many people do. But, like me, they're either too afraid or too polite to say so. That's why the movies are such a disaster. Now *there's* a form of popular culture that doesn't have a clue. Movies should be five minutes long. You should go in, see a couple of shots, maybe a room with orange draperies and a rug. A voice-over would say, "I'm having a hard time getting Raoul from the hotel room into the elevator." And, bang, that's the end. The lights come on, everybody walks out full of sympathy because this is a shared experience. Everybody in that theater knows how hard it is to get Raoul from the hotel room into the elevator. Everyone has had to do boring, dogged work. Everyone has lived a life that seems to inflict upon every vivid moment the smears, fingerings, and pawings of plot and feeling. Everyone has lived under this oppression. In other words, everyone has had to eat shit—day after day, the endless meals they didn't want, those dark, half-gelatinous lakes of gravy that lay on the plate like an ugly rug and that wrinkled clump of reddish-orange roast beef that looks like it was dropped onto your plate from a great height. God what a horror: getting Raoul into the elevator.

And that's why I write poetry. In poetry, you don't do that kind of work.

BODY AND SOUL *B. H. Fairchild*

Half-numb, guzzling bourbon and Coke from coffee mugs,
our fathers fall in love with their own stories, nuzzling
the facts but mauling the truth, and my friend's father begins
to lay out with the slow ease of a blues ballad a story
about sandlot baseball in Commerce, Oklahoma decades ago.
These were men's teams, grown men, some in their thirties
and forties who worked together in zinc mines or on oil rigs,
sweat and khaki and long beers after work, steel guitar music
whanging in their ears, little white rent houses to return to
where their wives complained about money and broken Kenmores
and then said the hell with it and sang *Body and Soul*
in the bathtub and later that evening with the kids asleep
lay in bed stroking their husband's wrist tattoo and smoking
Chesterfields from a fresh pack until everything was O.K.
Well, you get the idea. Life goes on, the next day is Sunday,
another ball game, and the other team shows up one man short.

They say, we're one man short, but can we use this boy,
he's only fifteen years old, and at least he'll make a game.
They take a look at the kid, muscular and kind of knowing
the way he holds his glove, with the shoulders loose,
the thick neck, but then with that boy's face under
a clump of angelic blonde hair, and say, oh, hell, sure,
let's play ball. So it all begins, the men loosening up,
joking about the fat catcher's sex life, it's so bad
last night he had to hump his wife, that sort of thing,
pairing off into little games of catch that heat up into
throwing matches, the smack of the fungo bat, lazy jogging
into right field, big smiles and arcs of tobacco juice,
and the talk that gives a cool, easy feeling to the air,
talk among men normally silent, normally brittle and a little
angry with the empty promise of their lives. But they chatter
and say rock and fire, babe, easy out, and go right ahead
and pitch to the boy, but nothing fancy, just hard fastballs
right around the belt, and the kid takes the first two
but on the third pops the bat around so quick and sure
that they pause a moment before turning around to watch
the ball still rising and finally dropping far beyond

the abandoned tractor that marks left field. Holy shit.
They're pretty quiet watching him round the bases,
but then, what the hell, the kid knows how to hit a ball,
so what, let's play some goddamned baseball here.
And so it goes. The next time up, the boy gets a look
at a very nifty low curve, then a slider, and the next one
is the curve again, and he sends it over the Allis Chalmers,
high and big and sweet. The left fielder just stands there, frozen.
As if this isn't enough, the next time up he bats left-handed.
They can't believe it, and the pitcher, a tall, mean-faced
man from Okarche who just doesn't give a shit anyway
because his wife ran off two years ago leaving him with
three little ones and a rusted-out Dodge with a cracked block,
leans in hard, looking at the fat catcher like he was the sonofabitch
who ran off with his wife, leans in and throws something
out of the dark, green hell of forbidden fastballs, something
that comes in at the knees and then leaps viciously towards
the kid's elbow. He swings exactly the way he did right-handed,
and they all turn like a chorus line toward deep right field
where the ball loses itself in sagebrush and the sad burnt
dust of dustbowl Oklahoma. It is something to see.

But why make a long story long: runs pile up on both sides,
the boy comes around five times, and five times the pitcher
is cursing both God and His mother as his chew of tobacco sours
into something resembling horse piss, and a ragged and bruised
Spalding baseball disappears into the far horizon. Goodnight,
Irene. They have lost the game and some painful side bets
and they have been suckered. And it means nothing to them
though it should to you when they are told the boy's name is
Mickey Mantle. And that's the story, and those are the facts.
But the facts are not the truth. I think, though, as I scan
the faces of these old men now lost in the innings of their youth,
I think I know what the truth of this story is, and I imagine
it lying there in the weeds behind that Allis Chalmers
just waiting for the obvious question to be asked: why, oh
why in hell didn't they just throw around the kid, walk him,
after he hit the third homer? Anybody would have,
especially nine men with disappointed wives and dirty socks
and diminishing expectations for whom winning at anything
meant everything. Men who knew how to play the game,

who had talent when the other team had nothing except this ringer
who without a pitch to hit was meaningless, and they could
    go home
with their little two-dollar side bets and stride into the house
singing *If You've Got the Money, Honey, I've Got the Time*
with a bottle of Southern Comfort under their arms and grab
Dixie or May Ella up and dance across the gray linoleum
as if it were V-Day all over again. But they did not.
And they did not because they were men, and this was a boy.
And they did not because sometimes after making love,
after smoking their Chesterfields in the cool silence and
listening to the big bands on the radio that sounded so glamorous,
so distant, they glanced over at their wives and noticed the lines
growing heavier around the eyes and mouth, felt what their wives
felt: that Les Brown and Glenn Miller and all those dancing
    couples
and in fact all possibility of human gaiety and light-heartedness
were as far away and unreachable as Times Square or the Avalon
ballroom. They did not because of the gray linoleum lying there
in the half-dark, the free calendar from the local mortuary
that said one day was pretty much like another, the work gloves
looped over the doorknob like dead squirrels. And they did not
because they had gone through a depression and a war that
    had left
them with the idea that being a man in the eyes of their fathers
and everyone else had cost them just too goddamned much to lay it
at the feet of a fifteen-year-old boy. And so they did not walk him,
and lost, but at least had some ragged remnant of themselves
to take back home. But there is one thing more, though it is not
a fact. When I see my friend's father staring hard into the
    bottomless
well of home plate as Mantle's fifth homer heads toward Arkansas,
I know that this man with the half-orphaned children and
worthless Dodge has also encountered for his first and possibly
only time the vast gap between talent and genius, has seen
as few have in the harsh light of an Oklahoma Sunday, the blonde
and blue-eyed bringer of truth, who will not easily be forgiven.

THE BRIDE OF FRANKENSTEIN *Edward Field*

The Baron has decided to mate the monster,
to breed him perhaps,
in the interests of pure science, his only god.

So he goes up into his laboratory
which he has built in the tower of the castle
to be as near the interplanetary forces as possible,
and puts together the prettiest monster-woman you ever saw
with a body like a pin-up girl
and hardly any stitching at all
where he sewed on the head of a raped and murdered beauty
    queen.

He sets his liquids burping, and coils blinking and buzzing,
and waits for an electric storm to send through the equipment
the spark vital for life.
The storm breaks over the castle
and the equipment really goes crazy
like a kitchen full of modern appliances
as the lightning juice starts oozing right into that pretty corpse.

He goes to get the monster
so he will be right there when she opens her eyes,
for she might fall in love with the first thing she sees as
    ducklings do.
That monster is already straining at his chains and slurping,
ready to go right to it:
He has been well prepared for coupling
by his pinching leering keeper who's been saying for weeks,
"Ya gonna get a little nookie, kid,"
or "How do you go for some poontang, baby?"
All the evil in him is focused on this one thing now
as he is led into her very presence.

She awakens slowly,
she bats her eyes,
she gets up out of the equipment,

and finally she stands in all her seamed glory,
a monster princess with a hairdo like a fright wig,
lightning flashing in the background
like a halo and a wedding veil,
like a photographer snapping pictures of great moments.

She stands and stares with her electric eyes,
beginning to understand that in this life too
she was just another body to be raped.

The monster is ready to go:

He roars with joy at the sight of her,
so they let him loose and he goes right for those knockers.
And she starts screaming to break your heart
and you realize that she was just born:
In spite of her big tits she was just a baby.

But her instincts are right—
rather death than that green slobber:
She jumps off the parapet.
And then the monster's sex drive goes wild.
Thwarted, it turns to violence, demonstrating sublimation
        crudely;
and he wrecks the lab, those burping acids and buzzing coils,
overturning the control panel so the equipment goes off like
        a bomb,
and the stone castle crumbles and crashes in the storm
destroying them all . . . perhaps.

Perhaps somehow the Baron got out of that wreckage of his
        dreams
with his evil intact, if not his good looks,
and more wicked than ever went on with his thrilling career.
And perhaps even the monster lived
to roam the earth, his desire still ungratified;
and lovers out walking in shadowy and deserted places
will see his shape loom up over them, their doom—
and children sleeping in their beds
will wake up in the dark night screaming
as his hideous body grabs them.

THE DIRTY FLOOR *Edward Field*

The floor is dirty:
Not only the soot from the city air
But a surprising amount of hair litters the room.
It is hard to keep up with. Even before
The room is all swept up it is dirty again.
We are shedding more than we realize.
The amount of hair I've shed so far
Could make sixty of those great rugs
The Duke of China killed his weavers for,
And strangle half the sons of Islam.
Time doesn't stop even while I scrub the floor
Though it seems that the mind empties like a bathtub,
That all the minds of the world go down the drain
Into the sewer; but hair keeps falling
And not for a moment can the floor be totally clean.
What is left of us after years of shitting and shedding?
Are we whom our mothers bore or some stranger now
With the name of son, but nameless,
Continually relearning the same words
That mean, with each retelling, less.
He whom you knew is a trail of leavings round the world.
Renewal is a lie: Who I was has no more kisses.
Barbara's fierce eyes were long ago swept up from her floor.
A stranger goes by the name of Marianne; it is not she,
Nor for that matter was the Marianne I knew.
The floor having accumulated particles of myself
I call it dirty; dirty, the streets thick with the dead;
I am alive at least. Quick, who said that?
Give me the broom. The leftovers sweep the leavings away.

OPEN SESAME *Edward Field*

. . . .

The door in the rock closed
just as he was about to enter.
His fingers even left imprints in the stone
where he gripped the panels,
straining against them as they slid together.
A minute more
and he would have gotten in.
Now he is almost embedded in the rock
arms outstretched
across the seamless face of it.

GRAFFITI *Edward Field*

. . . .

Blessings on all the kids who improve the signs in the subways:
They put a beard on the fashionable lady selling soap,
Fix up her flat chest with the boobies of a chorus girl,
And though her hips be wrapped like a mummy
They draw a hairy cunt where she should have one.

The bathing beauty who looks pleased
With the enormous prick in her mouth, declares
"Eat hair pie; it's better than cornflakes."
And the little boy in the Tarzan suit eating white bread
Now has a fine pair of balls to crow about.

And as often as you wash the walls and put up your posters,
When you go back to the caged booth to deal out change
The bright-eyed kids will come with grubby hands.
Even if you watch, you cannot watch them all the time,
And while you are dreaming, if you have dreams anymore,

A boy and girl are giggling behind an iron pillar;
And although the train pulls in and takes them on their way
Into a winter that will freeze them forever,
They leave behind a wall scrawled all over with flowers
That shoot great drops of gism through the sky.

MARVEL MYSTERY OIL *Elliot Fried*

No one knows what's in it, not even
the maker, but when I poured a quart
into my chattering V-8, it settled
right down and purred. When I tried it

on my wife's cooking, it improved
the taste tremendously, and then I
tried it on her. Now I use it
on my job, my friends. In a sense

I Mystery Oil my way through life.
It's slick with the smell of
Wintergreen, defeating friction
mysteriously. I used it

on this poem. If you do not
grasp it tightly, it will
slip from your fingers, slide
along the floor and out the door

into a world that needs lubrication
in the worst way. Marvel Mystery Oil.
It's better than religion.
A means of getting through.

WHY I WANT TO BE THE NEXT
POET LAUREATE *Elliot Fried*

I want to fiddle with a pipe and look profound,
plucking a mote of dust from my tweed sleeve
as I gaze into space, thinking thoughts so heavy
they sink into the ground. I want to have
a stern dog with pale silky hair that needs tending.
I want a frail consumptive woman, just a bit deranged,
waiting patiently in a dark room as I come home
after a hard day, flinging Guggenheim and Ford Foundation
grants onto the vacuumed shag. I want to write quatrains
for the sensitive. I want the thin crustless sandwiches
served by old ladies on polished silver trays . . .
I want the oolong tea. I want to suffer exquisitely
as I write of comely things: a cow upon a puffy hill,
the hazy gauze of sunset, a gull drifting in the misty air.
Most of all, Mark Strand, I want you to die
quickly though not necessarily painlessly, impaled, perhaps,
upon a rose bush or clipped by a Mack truck the color
of autumn smoke, or choked by a crustless sandwich. Get
the idea?

WORDSWORTH'S SOCKS *Elliot Fried*

. . . .

Hunched in the squat sleeper box of a black semi hurtling toward
Fresno, squirming on a thin foam pad, I suddenly thought of Words-
worth's socks, there in a clear fibreglass box in the Dove Cottage Mu-
seum. Inside, I'm getting tossed around the hot metal walls and out-
side the sun scarred hills that we're thundering past whisper BURN
ME, BURN ME, and I'm thinking of the socks, trying to remember
what they looked like, Wordsworth's Socks said the plaque beneath
and I remember thinking that if I stared at them long enough, they
would give me an insight into the entire Romantic Movement: Words-
worth and Coleridge sitting in that smoky house while Dorothy burnt
the dinner and outside the rain and mold clinging to the slate roof but
meanwhile the trucker up front is smoking a Camel and talking about
women and the clouds look like lumpy wool socks and I imagine Do-
rothy darning them in a cramped smoke filled room not even guess-
ing they'd end up in a museum behind Dove Cottage and the CB is
sputtering reports of accidents everywhere and down there in the
shimmering sticky heat is Fresno and a car to get me home but I can't
stop thinking of Wordsworth's socks and the statement they must
have made and I wonder why no pants no belt no shirt just socks but
Wordsworth's socks, his feet wrapped snugly inside, a poem inching
upward from the long prehensile toes and Fresno racing up, one long
ugly street with every convenience store in the universe stuck right
on it and the trucker stops his rig, turns to me, says this is it, this is
where you get off and I want to tell him about the socks, Wordsworth's
socks, in Dove Cottage Museum, but we're parked in front of
Granny's Chicken where on the roof a giant fibreglass elderly
chicken is laughing hysterically because it knows it's going to die but
then I bounce off the torn seat, stumble out the door and I'm gone,
keeping the image of Wordsworth's socks miraculously intact as I
wait on the corner for a cab, wondering can there be a poem in any
of this, and the answer, of course, is no.

This letter has been sent to you for good luck. The
original copy is in Muckluck, Australia. It has been
around the world nine times. You will receive good luck
in four days. This is no joke. You will receive it in the
mail. Send twelve copies of this letter. Do not keep it.
It must leave your hands within four days. Jack Ellman
received $60,000 and lost it when he broke the chain.
While in central Africa, Gene Mung received this letter
and failed to circulate it. His wife was eaten by ants.
This is no joke. Send out twenty copies of this letter
within two days. The chain comes from Cincinnati and
was written by Hiram Leech, a Bible salesman with
leprosy. Since the letter must make a tour of the world,
make one-hundred copies and send them out
immediately. After three days you will receive a
surprise. This is no joke. It is true even if you are not
superstitious. Note the following. Constantine Suarez
received this letter in 1953. He asked his secretary
to make two thousand copies and send them out. A few
days later he won a lottery of five million dollars. Andy
Dappit, an office employee, received this letter and
forgot it had to leave his hands within minutes. Two
days later he lost his fingers in a FAX machine. The
next week, after he sent out ten thousand copies, his
fingers returned. Send this letter now. Send it to everyone
in the world. It is probably already too late. This is no
joke.

DEB AT THE HAM SLICER *Cynthia Gallaher*

In California, she'd be a surfer girl,
but here in Chicago,
in this thick ethnic neighborhood,
she's a landlocked mermaid with bleach blond hair,
netted and enslaved at Neptune Discount.

I always know where to find her,
as I drop by during my own work break
from 8-Days-a-Week
Mini Mart next door;
Not aisle one,
where pink pearlescent nail polish
shimmers next to ghostly white lipsticks;
Not aisle two,
where washcloths, cheesecloth,
and dishrags lie silently
as army regalia
waiting for domestic wars;
Not aisle three,
the sad fluorescent-lit alley
of misbegotten parakeets and tri-color goldfish.

But there, in aisle four, Deb at the ham slicer,
her toned arms moving steel and blade
like a women's war poster from the 40s,
her shocking blond hair
veiled in the propriety
of a see-through hair net,
I barely move forward
when she spots me,
calls me by name
which echoes through the store,
Deb laughs loudly as a cheerleader,
but solemnly resumes slicing
as her boss approaches,
her face going into a trance,
reflecting dreams
of a someday built-in swimming pool,

a Tudor mansion and four-poster bed,
but at least by August,
the deepest tan possible
from her paint-peeled sun porch.

Deb is always tan, even in winter,
and the ham?
Slightly green around the edges,
year 'round.
Her boss tells her,
"If they buy it, sell it,"
while Deb continues to slice,
slice, slice,
the school year away.

Her shoes, Pappagallo,
the pantsuit beneath her smock,
Christian Dior,
the bracelets and rings
that jangle along the edges
of the ham slicer, 18 karat,
all ripped off from Marshall Field's
on her day off.
Deb keeps dreaming big,
slicing and selling meat,
saving her pennies
to position herself at a wealthy resort,
poolside, after graduation,
the glistening lifeguard
with Chanel behind her ears,
that pheromone for fools.

I heard she saved a young doctor
from drowning,
gave mouth-to-mouth
all pearly tooth and bronze,
her strong arms working him
like a warrior,
and when he came to,
she was selling it,
and he was buying it.

WHY I LEFT THE CHURCH *Richard Garcia*

Maybe it was
because the only time
I hit a baseball
it smashed the neon cross
on the church across
the street. Even
twenty-five years later
when I saw Father Harris
I would wonder
if he knew it was me.
Maybe it was the demon-stoked
rotisseries of purgatory
where we would roast
hundreds of years
for the smallest of sins.
Or was it the day
I wore my space helmet
to catechism? Clear plastic
with a red and white
inflatable rim.
Sister Mary Bernadette
pointed toward the door
and said, "Out! Come back
when you're ready."
I rose from my chair
and kept rising
toward the ceiling
while the children
screamed and Sister
kept crossing herself.
The last she saw of me
was my shoes disappearing
through cracked plaster.
I rose into the sky and beyond.
It is a good thing
I am wearing my helmet,
I thought as I floated
and turned in the blackness

and brightness of outer space.
My body cold on one side and hot
on the other. It would
have been very quiet
if my blood had not been
rumbling in my ears so loud.
I remember thinking,
Maybe I will come back
when I'm ready.
But I won't tell
the other children   ,
what it was like.
I'll have to make something up.

CHICKENS EVERYWHERE *Richard Garcia*

. . . .

You can't escape chickens. Chickens are all the rage. Alone in your car, you turn on the radio. It's The Chickens singing Glenn Miller's "In the Mood."

Even in your sleep there's no escape. You dream of a woman. She comes toward you opening her bathrobe. Between her legs, a chicken peeks out.

You are in the yard staring at your chicken. Your chicken is staring at you. Your chicken grows until it is six feet tall. You embrace. Never have you felt pleasure like this. You wake straddling your pillow.

You go to see your lady friend. She is wearing feathers. She moves her neck from side to side and clucks. It's no use. Walk alone in the night. Keep your collar up and your head down. The night is a chicken with enormous black wings. And you, little one, are a grain of wheat on the floor of a barn.

VERNON *Richard Garcia*

Vernon of brick smokestacks, of circuitous
slaughter houses, of meat packing, of heavy
and light industry, of wrong exits.
Vernon, where I found myself not
on the way to the airport.
Vernon, where the ribbon of concrete
that resembled the freeway entrance
was just the skeleton of a Roman aqueduct.
Vernon, where I slammed on my brakes,
effectively trapping the only pedestrian
in Vernon against a bridge railing.
"Do you know the way to the airport?" I said.
"Do you know the way to the airport?" he said,
apparently frightened into echolalia.
"No, but I do know the acrid smell of fear,"
I replied, as I sped off while watching him
mouth my words in the rearview mirror.
I thought of the murdered convict stuffed
into a fifty-gallon drum and shipped via UPS
to an animal rendering plant in Vernon.
VERNON, I cried out as I sped between warehouses
and self-storage facilities, as my wife's plane
flashed Fasten Seat Belts and flight attendants
were making sure all seats were in an upright position,
trays latched back, GOD HELP ME, I'M IN VERNON.
Vernon, a painting by de Chirico: a solitary tower,
an archway, shadows leaning against pylons,
a plaster face reflecting sunlight from the bottom
of a well representing an abyss of despair.
Vernon where I prayed my wife's plane would be late,
that she would step carefully from the hatch
through the rubbery mouth of a landing dock,
prepared to apologize for my long wait
and never know that I too had come vast distances
and emerged through a tunnel, had been face to face
with Vernon, my own private Vernon,
Vernon of no entrance, no exit, closed ramp,
under construction, detour, go back, severe tire damage.

MI MAMÁ, THE PLAYGIRL *Richard Garcia*

When my mother left Mexico, soldiers commandeered the train, forcing the passengers to get off and wait for the next one. Later they passed it lying on its side, burning.

She wore black dresses. Her closet was lined with identical pairs of black shoes. She constantly advised me to jump off the bridge while the tide was going out.

Long after my father was dead, she complained that his side of the bed still sank down. *"Viejo,"* she would tell him, "if you have somewhere to go, please go." At 70, she went out to nightclubs. Twisted her knee doing the bunny hop. Talked for hours to 40-year-old lovers on the phone. My brothers were ashamed.

After she died, she came to see me as she had promised. My father came, too. We sat around in the kitchen drinking coffee as if nothing had happened. My father looked great, said he'd been working out. She stroked his forearm, smiling at his tattoo of the dancing hula girl. When they left it was nothing dramatic. They just walked out the door and up a street that seemed to reach into the night sky. How beautiful, I thought, as I was waking, the stars shining in my mother's hair.

DEAR BOY GEORGE *Amy Gerstler*

. . . .

Only three things on earth seem useful or soothing to me.
One: wearing stolen clothes. Two: photos of exquisitely
dressed redheads. Three: your voice on the radio. Those songs
fall smack-dab into my range! Not to embarrass you with my
raw American awe, or let you think I'm the kinda girl who
bends over for any guy who plucks his eyebrows and can make
tight braids—but you're the plump bisexual cherub of the
eighties: clusters of Rubens' painted angels, plus a dollop of the
Pillsbury dough boy, all rolled into one! We could go skating,
or just lie around my house eating pineapple. I could pierce
your ears: I know how to freeze the lobes with ice so it doesn't
hurt. When I misunderstand your lyrics, they get even better.
I thought the line I'M YOUR LOVER, NOT YOUR RIVAL, was I'M
ANOTHER, NOT THE BIBLE, or PRIME YOUR MOTHER, NOT A LIBEL,
or UNDERCOVER BOUGHT ARRIVAL. Great, huh? See, we're of like
minds. I almost died when I read in the *Times* how you saved
that girl from drowning . . . dived down and pulled the blub-
bering sissy up. I'd give anything to be the limp, dripping
form you stumbled from the lake with, draped over your pale,
motherly arms, in a grateful faint, as your mascara ran and ran.

SLOWLY I OPEN MY EYES
(gangster soliloquy) *Amy Gerstler*

While the city sleeps there's this blast of silence that follows the whine of daylight: a defeat that wraps itself around buildings like a python, or one of those blue sheets they bundle corpses up in. Wanna go for an ambulance ride? Fragments of the sordid and the quote unquote normal vie for my attention. Hacking coughs and seductive yoo-hoos dangle in the 3 A.M. air. Up on this roof, I smoke cigarettes and wait. I feel like god up here. No kidding. Jerusalem Slim on his final night in the garden. Mr. X, Dr. No, The Invisible Man. All the same guy, different movies. It's a city of delinquents: my disciples. Maybe some bum down below finds one of my stubbed out butts and is delighted. Everybody's looking for something to inhale and something else to empty into. The whole city reels and twinkles at my feet, but the stars aren't impressed. They see it every night. The eighty-year-old elevator operator downstairs snores like he's trying to suck up the Hudson. Humans act as if they're going to stick around forever, but nobody ever does. That's what cracks me up.

AN UNEXPECTED ADVENTURE *Amy Gerstler*

Driving home to River Heights after a hard day's work on a new mystery, Nancy Drew's dark blue roadster lurches, and slows. "A flat, I'll bet." Nancy's hunches are spooky: she's almost always right. The young sleuth pulls onto the gravel shoulder, removes her gloves, places her handbag on the seat beside her. Night is falling. Cunningly attired in a simple two-piece linen sports frock with matching sweater, the girl detective changes the tire easily. Though she doesn't relish the work, she's no shirker, and the convertible is soon repaired. Nancy's pooped, so at first she doesn't notice the short, heavy-set man with a large nose approaching. But nothing escapes Nancy's keen gaze for long. "That fellow acts as if he's being pursued," Nancy notes. Her eyes sparkle with anticipation. Her intuition tells her she may be on the threshold of another mystery! As the man draws closer, Nancy controls her excitement, and speaks in a calm, casual voice: "Sir, may I offer you some assistance?" she asks sincerely.

Even after repairing her car, Nancy looks incredibly clean. Her sports frock is perfectly tailored to her trim figure. The color suits her complexion exactly. The creamy pallor of her skin contrasted with the healthy flush of recent exertion still fresh on her cheeks is very becoming. The stranger's face descending toward hers and his unpleasant breath are the last items to register clearly on the amateur detective's mind as his stout, red, puffy hands find her sweater clasp. Nancy's miffed when she comes to, lying alone in the road. The culprit's vanished. She notices immediately her purse is gone, and with it her car keys. Her intuition clicking like a geiger counter, she has a revelation she may have lost more than her compact and billfold to this ruffian, as, with leaden feet, she begins the long walk home.

ARS POETICA *John Gilgun*

About writing a poem. It occurs to me
That in a good one
There should be a startling "something"
Coming at you out of nowhere
Like the rusted-out pickup
That's about to smash into you
On the Belt Highway
Coming at you out of the corner
Of the rearview mirror
Or out of the corner of your eye
Or out of the corner of your eye reflected
(Oh God!) in the rearview mirror.
Look, Cesar Vallejo does it!
Not smash into you in a pickup on the Belt,
I mean, but toss something at you
That rearranges your brain.
A real mental flip-out,
That's what you want.
You also want to work in allusions
To Vallejo,
The way I just did.
Or to Basho or Akhmatova.
If they're Chilean, Japanese or Russian,
Go for it, man!
And you want a pinch of mystery,
Again as with Vallejo. For instance,
"Y no saben que el Misterio sintetiza,"
Which means,
"They don't know that the Mystery joins
All things together."
Like, "Why was I born, why am I living?"
You know, that old song. "To love you."
And love, that's a good subject for poetry,
But you can't just come out in favor of it.
You have to be sneaky about it as in,
"Love may be great, but as for me . . ."
Then you can prove that it's great,
Though, to tell the truth, it's not,

Not all the time anyway.
As for models, go directly to Frank O'Hara.
Do not pass Go, do not collect a hundred dollars
From the Poetpourri's Annual Summer Sizzler Contest
Sponsored by the Comstock Writers' Group
in Syracuse, New York.
Frank O'Hara may have written this poem
For all you know. Can you prove that he didn't?
Then, finally, it's important
To put your friends in your poem,
As O'Hara knew.
After all, your friends will probably be
With you at Lulu's in Kansas City
The night you read your poem
And you want them to remain your friends,
Right? So—
"Hans, Jeff, Tony, Scott, Roger, Mike . . ."
As for an ending for your poem,
The ending should have nothing to do with
Anything that went before,
As with James Wright's poem
About sleeping in the hammock
On William Duffy's farm.
Remember, where he says,
"I have wasted my life!"
And it has nothing to do with
Butterflies and horse manure?
So I'm going to end my poem with,
"Perhaps by your motions my body is healed."
Now it's seven o'clock in the morning,
May 11, 1992,
And I have to take a shower, get dressed
And go to work. Thank you very much,
Don't mention it! Hey!

TALKING ABOUT BOYS *Lisa Glatt*

Once you've had one boy you can imagine all the rest. You can stand with other girls like you—and you can talk. You can gather in places like bathrooms and fix your face, rubbing, patting, and you can say, Boys, ha, I know all about them. You can nod your head. You can sigh. You can pout with them and complain, discussing what the boys do and do not do. And you can lie, inventing stories in the locker room, as the boys themselves do, standing in their boxers, boasting. You can stand in your bra and silk panties, discussing them—the sizes of boys, how their penises are shaped—do not worry, once you've seen one boy you've seen most of the rest as well—unless of course your boy was uncircumcised.

You must look for a certain type of girl, a certain group of girls, with whom to discuss boys. The others will not respond the way you'd like. The others—say a cheerleader or a churchgoer or a girl in pastels— might condemn you. A churchgoing cheerleader in pastels is to be particularly avoided. Whatever she asks of you, say no. Volleyball? No. Breakfast on Sunday? No. Dinner at her house with her father the minister? Absolutely not. Run from her. Go to the nearest mall or 7- Eleven or Donny's Donuts. They'll be standing outside, these girls, propped against a wire fence. They may be smoking. They will be brooding. Several of their bellies will be on display, a button or two pierced. Creep up, join them, and start talking.

THE WORLD IN MY MOTHER'S HAIR *Lisa Glatt*

. . . .

My mother hates her life
and dyes her hair—nearly daily, at least
three or four times a week. I call
and she says, "Call me back. I'm right
in the middle of a new color—Burnt Ruby."

My mother hates her life
and believes that Burnt Ruby will bring her man back
to the bedroom, on his knees,
with the word yes
on his hot, red tongue.

My mother imagines his return
will change things—the way
I see her: At noon with a cup of tea
sitting on the plaid couch
with one hand on the cat and the other
shaking as she reaches for the cup—
in the evening with her head
bent over the kitchen sink,
with the douche-like bottle
poised, with her scalp
burning, with her scalp
pleading, with her scalp
and all of its demands.

My mother thinks
his return
will cure her hypertension,
will cheer the cat,
will make the neighbors
take notice of her shiny hair.

LEASH *Lisa Glatt*

Did I tell you I wanted one of those leashes you see at the mall,
the ones the mothers wrap around their toddlers' waists
so that the toddlers will not wander?
But I was thirty when I wanted a leash like that
and I wanted to follow her anywhere: work, theaters,
Las Vegas with her friends, even into that midnight morning.
When she vomited I felt the bile rise in my own sad belly.
And when she moaned I moaned.
And when she died I stood by the bed
and was still here.

LIFE IS HAPPY, *Albert Goldbarth*

I suddenly understand: I'm watching you chop away
at a cabbage, you're humming, the kitchen is light
and knife-thrust, light and knife-thrust,
lightslaw, airslaw, and humming. That would be the way
Life gets its blade out, then goes at it
with a human heart: maybe like somebody hacking
jungle undergrowth, so the whole heart's lost in a minute,
ribbons, pulp; or maybe making all exquisite show
of almond-like slivers, holding up
the fussy ricegrain-sized inscribings, studying
its artistry from many angles, taking years,
taking seventy years; but humming
in an absentminded, pleasurable way, no matter
the time involved, or what the technique—happy. This
was the lesson, now I remember, carried by the moted light
of the bulky, asthmatically-purring projector
they used for grade school "nature films." The room
was darkened, our tittering hushed, and then a voice,
a grave yet understanding, deeply male voice, came forth
from that machine, while on the screen a grainy lion
brought a grainy zebra down, and this was followed
by a few frames of its running with the bowel. This
was "the law of the jungle," "the law of fang and claw," and
so we understood that what we saw
as horrifying slaughter—and that zebra's widened jaws
and splayed gray teeth would bray inside my brain
for years—was part of a governing system, a balance:
there was pain, but it was ordered pain, and Life
was in the greenish jungle vapor, or the sky, all the while,
surveying its handiwork, calmly. Not *a life*, but Life
was happy, standing grandly in the kitchen
with its tools and its purview, neither king nor cabbage
more endeared to it, the knife out, at some moments
even looking like love, its hair, its hips,
its smooth, assumed efficiency,
its dearly off-key humming.

THE SCIENCES SING A LULLABYE *Albert Goldbarth*

Physics says: go to sleep. Of course
you're tired. Every atom in you
has been dancing the shimmy in silver shoes
nonstop from mitosis to now.
Quit tapping your feet. They'll dance
inside themselves without you. Go to sleep.

Geology says: it will be alright. Slow inch
by inch America is giving itself
to the ocean. Go to sleep. Let darkness
lap at your sides. Give darkness an inch.
You aren't alone. All of the continents used to be
one body. You aren't alone. Go to sleep.

Astronomy says: the sun will rise tomorrow,
Zoology says: on rainbow-fish and lithe gazelle,
Psychology says: but first it has to be night, so
Biology says: the body-clocks are stopped all over town
and
History says: here are the blankets, layer on layer, down and down.

MY RODEO   *Jack Grapes*

I'm ashamed of my cheap rodeo
so I keep it secret from my friends.
It's not even as big as theirs
and needs constant repair.
"How's your rodeo?" someone asks at a party.
"Fine!" they chirp up.
They jump at the chance
to extol the virtues of their rodeo.
Pretty soon a circle gathers
and everyone's discussing its size,
weather control, the acoustics, the peanuts.
If I stay in my corner someone will notice and ask about mine.
I don't want to talk about it.
So I join in, chirping up with you-don't-says, and isn't-that-amazings
and what-about-the-functional-glitter?
By the time I get home
I'm exhausted from avoiding the subject of my rodeo.
I get home and there it is,
not much on weather control, lousy acoustics,
styrofoam peanuts.
There's no sub-culture, no glitz-trimming,
no contour illuminations, not even jacket hitch
where the top bolt exceeds the maintenance quota lining.
I'm embarrassed and ashamed of the damn thing,
give it a kick and stub my toe, then cover it with a sheet.
Maybe smother it.
I am a man who comes home depressed, lonely,
frustrated, who tries to smother his rodeo,
his cheap rodeo.
And I haven't even the courage to do that.
Imagine smothering one's rodeo.
The shame would haunt me the rest of my life.
So after awhile I take the sheet off and go to bed,
hearing its slight breathing throughout the night,
its occasional cough, the short low moan
just before daybreak. My cheap rodeo.

LISTEN *Jack Grapes*

Listen, what are you reading this for?
Haven't you got bills to pay,
a movie you've been wanting to see,
a woman to love or a wife to ignore.
I'm here because it's raining,
and poets write poems when it rains—
at least that's what I read once somewhere.
(Listen, I'm lying to you. It's not raining.
I just said that because it sounded good.
It's a beautiful day. There's liable to be a law
or a proverb dealing it a blow from which
it may never recover that's how beautiful a day
it is and you should find a girl or a football
and a field of clover
to take them both
around around around.)

Are you reading this to feel better?
Do you think writing this makes me feel better?
Let me tell you something.
You know what'll make me feel better?
A million dollars. A million million dollars.
I want to be corrupted by money and fame
so bad it squeaks my socks.
I want to be filthy with money
to buy filthy men out
and sell their souls
for a bucket of paint.
I want to have so much money
I'll be able to rob my own bank,
buy my way in and out of jail,
cook omelettes from golden goose's eggs,
send every starving poet
a twenty dollar cook book
and laugh in their faces
saying:

I don't need your words!
I don't need your poems!
I don't need your books or your dreams.
I don't need your aches and pains
and sensational sufferings!
I don't need your visions
your eyes your goddamn poet's eyes!
I've Got Money, Baby!
I'VE GOT ALL THE MONEY
IN THE WORLD!
I OWN THE EARTH AND THE SUN
AND THE PLANETS
AND THE STARS I DON'T OWN,
NO ONE CAN BUY!
I CAN BE GOD! I CAN BE GOD!

———————

Listen, I didn't mean what I wrote.
I got a little carried away.
You'll forgive me because it's raining.
I get carried away when it rains.
I don't want money.
I don't want power.
I don't want to own men's souls.
I want just to be a poet.
To write words of startling beauty
to fill the universe
of emptiness
in your soul.
To make the trees dance
and the winds curl back upon themselves
like confetti off a ship.

I want your tears.
I want to reach
the depth of such beauty—
I want the universe to suffer
because beauty is a pain beyond pain
that dies in the willow

as well as in the wars of men.
I want all men to own my soul,
the poet's soul,
for it's always for the asking.
I want to belong to all the nations,
and all the oceans.
I want to belong to the earth,
the planets,
all the stars,
and all the spaces
beyond all spaces.
I want to be god.

I LIKE MY OWN POEMS *Jack Grapes*

I like my own poems
best.
I quote from them
from time to time
saying, "A poet once said,"
and then follow up
with a line or two
from one of my own poems
appropriate to the event.
How those lines sing!
All that wisdom and beauty!
Why it tickles my ass
off its spine.
"Why those lines are mine!"
I say
and Jesus, what a bang
I get out of it.

I like the ideas in them,
my poems,
ideas that hit home.
They speak to me.
I mean, I understand
what the hell
the damn poet's
talking about.

"Why I've been there,
the same thing," I shout,
and Christ! What a shot it is,
a shot.

And hey.
The words!
Whew!
I can hardly stand it.
Words sure do not fail
this guy, I say.

From some world
only he knows
he bangs the bong,
but I can feel it
in the wood,
in the wood of the word,
rising to its form
in the world.
"Now, you gotta be good
to do that!" I say
and damn! It just shakes
my heart,
you know?

THE CASE AGAINST MIST *Mark Halliday*

He could not be just particles of mist
dispersing into the sky, he could not be only that
and there are many reasons.
There are some reasons why.

For example, he paddled a canoe down the Housatonic River
for nineteen miles
and learned to keep up with some considerably stronger boys
and then they all laughed together over blueberry pancakes
and that is a reason why.

Also he wrote quite unhappily about the failure of Reconstruction
during the presidency of Ulysses S. Grant,
frowning at the exam booklet in a hot overlit room,
forming complete sentences though he could not remember
anything about Jay Gould, sincerely wishing
he could remember more facts
and sincerely sorry to disappoint Mr. Bennett
and this would not be true if he were simply
particles of mist drifting up into the infinite sky
and so that is why.

Also he never forgot the pathos of sexual fear
which would always link a certain song by Fontella Bass
with a certain large girl in a stiff green dress
in an old Volvo on such a dark highway near Rowayton.
Clearly, thus, he could not be just particles of mist.
The proof is right there.

Besides, his mother sang "Let's go together, says Pooh to me,
let's go together says Pooh" and she sang this
just for him in a voice better than anything else.
So there is a huge proof.

Not to mention that he showed real kindness
to some lonely and troubled individuals
in several houses, lobbies, cafeterias, train stations and
municipal parks, probably to more than 20 percent

of those lonely and anxious individuals that he actually met
in those places during his long busy life, true kindness
with money or food, or talk, or at least thoughtful gestures
and all this constitutes another reason why,
why he could in no way be just mist, vapor, molecules
well on their way to dispersion and nothing else.

We see thus that the proofs are many
and still more could be adduced,
though any one of them should have been enough.

CREDENTIALS *Mark Halliday*

He has never lost a child. He has never even
almost lost a child. How can he talk about loss?
He has never been raped. Not even almost raped.
How can he expect us to listen? He has never been
beaten bloody by his father or anyone else.
He has never watched a relative or friend die in agony
or even quietly, yet. (Except his mother long ago and
so slowly.) How can he presume? Why should he stand up
and speak of suffering, or grief? He has never seen anyone
get shot or stabbed in real life. He has never been mugged
or even almost mugged. (The one time he was burglarized,
the event was small and absurd in the tomato-stained
banality of South Philadelphia.) He has never
jumped from a burning house. Did he once survive tornado,
earthquake, flood? Absolutely not. And he sure as hell
never crouched in a fucking jungle ditch while fucking
AK-47 bullets sprayed mud on his fucking helmet.
How does he think he can talk about fear?
He was never tortured by the police of Paraguay
or even arrested in Turkey. He has never spent a single night
in jail. He is practically a stranger to severe pain
(the exceptions were brief) and terrible danger.
He has never tried heroin or even cocaine.
Never did he slit his wrists or even think about it.
In a way the man has barely lived! Yet still
he solicits our attention when we could be listening
to those who have truly suffered. Does he think
everyone has a serious truth? Does he know what modesty is?
Does he think nothing matters but "language"?
Does he regard metaphor as a wardrobe to dress up
triviality? Does he not see
that we couldn't listen to every sad story
even if we wanted to?

MY MORAL LIFE *Mark Halliday*

Two years hence. When I'm ready.
After one more set of poems
about my beautiful confusion.
After I've read *Anna Karenina*
and *Don Quixote*
and the first volume at least of Proust
and one big novel by Thomas Mann—
say three years. Three years hence:

after I've written an essay about the word "enough"
and after I've done something so delectable
weaving together phrases from Henry James and Bob Dylan
and after I've written an amazing meditation on Luis Buñuel
and after I've spent a month in Frankfort, Michigan
being very real and thoughtful and full of perspective
and fresh cherry pie
then—
then—

in four years at the most—
I see it there ahead of me casting a silver shadow
back upon me now, bathing me in its promise,
validating the self that will arrive at it
in four years or less (maybe just two years?) . . .
Glimpsing it there is sometimes like already living it
almost and feeling justifiably proud.
Water pollution and toxic waste and air pollution;
the poverty of black people in my city;
the nuclear arms industry; in my moral life these things
are not just TV, they push my poems to the edge of my desk,
they push Henry James into a sweet corner,
they pull me to meetings and rallies and marches
and meetings and rallies and marches.
There I am in a raincoat on the steps of City Hall
disappointed by the turnout but speaking firmly
into the local news microphone about the issue,

the grim issue.
When I'm ready.
Four years from today!
Silver shadow

INVENTION *Barbara Hamby*

I am personally indebted to antiquity because if it were left
to me nothing would have been invented. We would still be chasing

boars and clubbing them to death. No, that's too refined.
We'd still be eating grass and grubbing for worms.

How did they think up all that stuff? I'm not talking
about painting or literature or music. That's easy.

What could be more natural than sitting around a campfire
telling stories and then rhyming to make them easier to remember

or having two or three people take different parts?
Voila, poetry and theatre. I'm talking about bread.

Who thought of grinding wheat and mixing it with mold?
Forget bread. I can't get past wheat. Wheat must have been a weed

once. Who walked up to wheat and thought about growing
a whole field of it, picking it, smashing it together,

adding water, throwing it on a fire? Who were these
proto-chemists, these Neanderthal Marie and Pierre Curies

who harnessed the grain? The leap from throwing rocks at birds
and grilling them on a spit to Safeway is too great for me,

which leads to another subject if one picks up reading material
in supermarkets. Recently I discovered that alien civilizations

do not vacation on Earth anymore because we are too bellicose
and vulgar. Well, whose fault is it anyway? Anyone who thinks

that buffoons such as we could have thought up wheat,
not to mention architecture, axles, armor, artillery

is not taking his Lithium. There would still be about 250 of us
in caves somewhere in France if someone with big silver eyes

hadn't been buzzing around the universe, bored, sentimental,
and decided to stop and help us along. Next thing you know

there's agriculture, horticulture, apiculture. It's the only
logical explanation and if it weren't for the CIA,

everyone would agree with me. However, scientists in Russia,
Argentina, and the north of England (top-notch men,

every one of them) theorize that not only did the Andromedans
show us a few tricks, they also mated with the indigenous

species. Yuck, you might say, if they think we're creepy now,
just imagine what our manners were like ten or twenty thousand

years ago, though come to think of it, I doubt the alien *haute
bourgeoisie* was patrolling the outer reaches of the universe.

According to a test devised by these scientists, you can tell
if you are descended from extraterrestrials by certain physical

characteristics, such as blond hair, slender fingers,
musical ability (especially singing), big eyes, blue eyes,

which all point to a racially pure colony in Sweden
or Schleswig-Holstein for a few thousand years

and are somewhat reminiscent of our recent troubles in Europe
and Japan. I, for one, would like to toast an inventor:

Tchin, tchin, Dom Perignon, who said when he discovered
champagne, "My God, I am drinking the stars."

MR. PILLOW *Barbara Hamby*

I'm watching a space invasion movie in which a wife
tells her pilot husband that she hugs his pillow

when he is away. Well, sure, every girl does that,
takes comfort in Mr. Pillow when her boyfriend is gone,

but not when Bela Lugosi is breaking the lock
on your prefab fifties bungalow. You fight him off,

but he still knows where you are, and the police don't care,
or they're bumbling incompetents, and your husband is big

but not too bright; let's face it, he's not even a pilot,
he's an actor and not a very good one at that,

and what Mr. Pillow lacks in facial definition,
he more than makes up for in his cuddle quotient,

although there is the genital dilemma. Poor Mr. Pillow
is sadly lacking in that area. I hate staying in hotels

because of the king-size beds. I did not get married
not to sleep with my husband. If I had, Mr. Pillow

would do just as well, because he's certainly never sarcastic
and he'd let me run my credit cards up as high as I want

and never make me save for retirement, so I have to admit
that I have, on occasion, used Mr. Pillow to make my husband

jealous, as when he's sitting on his side of an enormous
hotel bed, way over in a far island of dull yellow

lamplight, reading a fascinating article on flyfishing
in Antarctica or the destruction of life as we know it

on Planet Earth, and I turn to Mr. Pillow, hold him tight
and say, "Oh, Mr. Pillow, you know what a woman needs

from a man." Getting no response from the outer reaches
of Patagonia, I whisper, "Oh, Mr. Pillow, you make me blush."

"Would you shut up about Mr. Pillow?" "Oh, Mr. Pillow!"
I say as he flies across the room, and I get just what I want

and maybe what I deserve. Sometimes it's so difficult
to make these distinctions. Puritanism dies hard,

and if there are ghouls lurking in the yard, who's to say
they have any less right to be here than we do in our cozy

little beds all the while looking at the closet door, thinking,
Where are the cannibals, where do those zombies live?

BERIBERI *Barbara Hamby*

For five or six years I haven't been really emotional,
I mean rip-roaring mad. Where did my anger go?

Did I lose it one afternoon walking home from work
or misplace it as my grandmother once did her teeth,

later finding them in the pantry behind cans of beans?
The nearest I come to emotion these days is panic,

as when the pilot of our plane tried to land
in the middle of Tropical Storm Beryl. For God's sake,

it had a name. Don't they have a rule in pilot school?
Rule number 437? You idiot, if a storm has a name,

don't try to land. When we touched down the first time,
the woman behind me said, "Thank you, Jesus,"

which quickly turned into, "Oh, my God,"
because we went right back up only to try it again,

the plane shaking like a little girl with fire ants
in her shoes. I have never been so aware of my own heart,

how small it is, how hard it works. All the way back to Tampa,
I listened to my body toil like a farmer in the fields,

each breath plowing through my lungs and into the blood
like an iron blade, each thought painful, not dead

but not really alive either. In my younger days
I was quite the little Sturm-und-Dranger. I remember

when we were first married, that fight we had.
There were so many rules, and I didn't seem to know

any of them, so one day I snapped and stalked
through the house apologizing: I'm sorry, I beg

your pardon, Excuse me, Forgive me, It's my fault,
Oh, I *am* a dunce, How can you bear it, living

with such a moron? My boyfriend had turned into
Family Man, which involved meal planning, child care,

and IRAs and I'm not talking about the Irish group
that blows up train stations. More than anything

I wanted my boyfriend back. What evil spirit
made you become that voodoo Ward Cleaver who suddenly

wanted to act married? Then something changed, both of us,
I suppose, because you are your beautiful self again.

Did we break a mirror or eat potato salad
that had been too long in the sun? Be careful, darling.

I know I say it too much. When you leave the house
without me, who will watch for the odd malevolent truck,

falling trees, the lightning? From Paris, Madame de Sévigné
wrote to her daughter in Provence: "My dear,

I must be persuaded of your real affection for me
since I am still alive." Wretched hours that separate us,

as if an essential nutrient were missing, as in the deficiency
of vitamin B1, a disease characterized by great weakness

and called beriberi, which translated is, "I cannot."
I cannot imagine a greater pleasure than to lie in bed

at night and listen to you breathe, the dark room around me
like a veil. Sometimes I wake and wonder if I am dead,

but I must be alive since you are breathing and your heart
is beating, filled with blood, empty, then full again.

THE INTELLIGENCE QUOTIENT *Deborah Harding*

When I read the article about phenobarbital
lowering the IQs of children
I wondered if I was one of them.
Back in 1960, when I was six, I took them
three times a day, like clockwork—
teeny, white, harmless pills
to stop the seizures. For seven years
I popped them like a little trooper
to keep the bad spells away—
sudden jerk of my bottom jaw
wagging like a loose hinge, the cold
froth of saliva starting to build
as those slurred sounds
sputtered off my tongue. I remember
falling once as if in slow motion
from the kitchen chair, hard slap
of linoleum against my cheek,
close blur of their faces.
I remember the spinal tap, the green
pull of the ether, and the EEG,
mysterious band of pin pricks
biting my scalp. That was the worst of it,
or so I thought—But what if slowly
I'd been getting dumber and dumber,
that white powder dissolving like Kool-Aid
stunting my math scores, what if I
really had been as smart as
Katy Henderson before I turned junkie,
maybe even gifted, my cortex
a compressed hive buzzing with know-how—
What a different life it might have been,
no nose to the grindstone
no tutors, but a girl brimming with confidence,
knowing what she knows,
intelligence rolling sweet as honey
off my tongue into their ears
pricked dumb in amazement.

DON'T CHEAPEN YOURSELF *Jana Harris*

You look sleazy tonight,
ma said.
Cheap, I said,
I'm doin cheap.
You got any idea
how much it costs
to do cheap these days?
To do gold City of Paris
three-inch platform sandals
and this I. Magnin snake dress?
I'm doin cheap.
You look like a bird, she said,
a Halloween bird with red waxed lips.
    —In high school
you could either do cheap or Shakespeare,
college prep or a pointy bra,
ratting a bubble haircut
with a toilet brush.
I was not allowed to do high school cheap,
I did blazers and wool skirts
from the Junior League thrift shop.
In high school it was
don't walk in the middle of
Richie, Leelee, and the baby,
you might come between them.
You look like a skag
wearin that black-eyed makeup,
people are gonna think you're cheap.
While I poured red food dye
on my hair
to match my filly's tail for the rodeo,
ma beat her head against the wall,
she said
trying to make me nice.
I tried real hard,
but the loggers, the Navy guys,
they always hit on me.

Cause you're an easy mark, ma said.
And I played guilty,
I played guilty every time.
But now, I said,
now I'm doin cheap.

BENEATH THE POLE OF PROUD RAVEN *Jana Harris*

She said, Creek Daughter
give me your gray gray hair,
creek daughter, give me
the glacier water,
—gray hair, cold water—
give me their child, creek daughter
give me the fish, creek daughter
give me your gray gray hair

She said, Fish
give me your silver skin, fish
give me your silver silver skin
give me your silver salmon skin
fish, give me your skin

She said, Loon
give me your noise, loon
give me your high pitched crazed call
give me your loon-call echoing
off the island rocks, loon
give me your noise, loon
give me your noise

She said, Wolf
tired wolf, tired swimming wolf
give me your claws, tired wolf
give me your claws

She said, Crow
give me your coat, crow
give me your raven down coat
give me your coat like night,
crow, give me the night, crow
give me your coat

She said, Woman
give me the fog, woman
give me the fog, give me

the spruce-root hat where
you've hidden the fog
woman, give me the fog

She said, Coals
give me the fire spirit, coals
give me your pitch-stick smell,
give me your spruce-gum smoke
coals, give me the fire spirit

She said, Whale
give me your bones, blackfin
give me their slopes and hills,
bring me the mountains, whale
give me your bones

She said, Creek Daughter
give me your gray gray hair
give me the glacier water
She said, Fish
give me your silver silver skin
She said, Loon
give me your noise, loon
She said, Wolf
tired swimming wolf
give me your claws
She said, Crow
give me your coat like night
She said, Woman
give me the fog
She said, Coals
give me the fire spirit
She said, Whale
give me your bones, blackfin
bring me the mountains

She said,
I am the glacier
She said,
I am the fish
She said,

I am the loon
She said,
I am the wolf
She said,
I am the night
She said,
I am the fog
She said,
I am the fire
She said,
I am the mountain
She said,
I am the power
She said,
I am the earth
She said,

Beware

THE POPE AT 7:00 P.M. *Eloise Klein Healy*

Does the Pope sit alone
with a china plate of spumoni
and a glass of white wine?

When it is all quiet
from theology,
does he read humility reports
from Mother Superiors
or check the scholastic progress
of native clergy from African places?

Does the Pope think on charity
and decide to give away
what the Vatican reaps?
At 7:15 does he think
of the library's collection
of pornographic literature?
Does he wonder if he could
give it away?

Does he ever eat too much
lasagna or spill
sauce on his small white shoes?

At 7:45 does he want to get undressed?
Does the Pope have pajamas,
a nightshirt, or nothing?
If he's sleepy does he nod
and tip his glass
or must he read to fall asleep?

Does he read in American or Latin,
or does he have a clock alarm
from somebody
as a present?
Or a television—
does the Pope know

146

the Dating Game?
Or does he just sit
there in the quiet
wondering what other people do?

Radio about a foot-and-a-half
wide swinging at his side.
Three boys abreast and one
has the radio playing loud rock
they talk to as they walk
past my house. Three boys
dressed in their style
of short jackets and caps pulled
down almost to their eyes.
They might as well be naked
boys in the hot sun singing
in a changing boy voice the songs
they like to hear. They might
as well be boys chipping rocks
into weapons or tools.
But they are only boys on the way
someplace. They have to be men
sometime and no time for idle
rambling to rock music unless
they take jobs in the outdoors
where they can still be boys
and dress to get dirty. They can
be boys underneath the culture
forever because some other man
will gladly take those boys
and chip them down into tools
or weapons or bake them into
the walls of his own idea
of empire.

ADVICE LIKE THAT *Eloise Klein Healy*

The woman had the boy by the hand.
He was maybe nine years old. He was dirty.
His mouth was smeared and his stomach stuck out
where his shirt ended and his pants began.
She had on a cloth coat. We all had that kind
in the '6os like Jackie Kennedy. A nappy texture,
but this one sagged from its shoulders, her shoulders.

She held the boy out to me and said could I give
her something so she and her baby
could have breakfast.
I gave her a dollar. She smiled. No teeth on the right side.
She looked me up and down. *Honey*, she said,
them wind things blowing in the road,
don't walk through them no more.

She and the boy went to Burrito King.
I drove out to the Valley to my therapist.
A dollar is little to spend for advice like that.

it was gonna be his ticket home just a flesh wound you know like those TV detectives always got a clean hole punched through soft tissue no veins or arteries no real damage but enough to take him to the rear some base hospital with pretty nurses and a real bed with sheets hot food hot water maybe even a bathtub soak them humpin'-the-boonies blues away had it all figured out wait till almost dark sittin' on the edge of his foxhole cleaning rag out weapon pointed down muzzle near his calf say it went off accidental while he was tryin' to figure why it'd been jammin' everybody knew M-16s jammed just point and squeeze sure it'd hurt a little but it'd be better than waitin' for Charlie to put one through his head that'd happen soon he'd dreamed it some sniper sightin' down the back of his brain ready to turn his skull into some kinda Humpty Dumpty jigsaw puzzle pieces scattered like bloody egg shell all over a rice paddy berm this was better just exhale and squeeze real soft blam clean little hole and home free nobody could expect him to go humpin' a rucksack with a hole through his leg at the least he'd get assigned to the rear limp real good for a few months till he was so short it wouldn't matter maybe it'd be better if he closed his eyes come on you're not gonna make it out here you know it just do it think of that nice tub of steamin' water sweet-smellin' Ivory soap home just squeeze

MEMORY *Bob Hicok*

. . . .

I hated the Road Runner.
I hated the Road Runner almost as much
as catching my father's knuckle ball.
And for whatever reason
these two displeasures became joined at the hip,
siamese tortures which still appear from time to time
on my psychic horizon.
TV's usually the trigger,
a chance encounter with the cartoon,
the theme song lodging in my cerebellum,
medulla oblongata
or whatever cranial nook it is
that absorbs the snatches of tunes
which loop us to insanity.
"Road Runner, the Coyote's after you.
Road Runner, if he catches you you're through."
Then I see the ball's
psychotic approach, the sphere jumping,
popping, weaving toward my shins or knees or thighs
or yes, higher still, so I can tell you
the joke about such an event creating a momentary soprano's
a lie, because each time I was too engrossed in moaning
to speak, let alone sing,
and would have been satisfied to live out my life
a monk, with a vocabulary of nods and gestures and safe
from the gonadal dangers of sport.
Memories often link umbilically.
Disraeli couldn't hear Big Ben without thinking of treacle.
I've a friend
who each time a jet flies by
remembers Miss Horton, his first grade teacher,
and her passion for the hokey pokey.
I thought of these things while reading about a man
imprisoned by mistake.
In the article he mentioned
the ten years of his wife's hard kisses he'd missed,
a son shot gunned in a drive-by
and the guards' refusal

to give him his suit and money back,
making him walk out of court in prison blues, broke
but staring into a free man's sunshine.
At home he took his blue three-piece,
blue jeans, even his blue socks
to the back yard, poured gas on the pile
and lit it with his brother's Zippo.
But it didn't work, he continued,
because any little thing
makes me remember, makes me feel
like I'm still in the joint, just another nigger
owned by time. The interviewer then asked
what he recalled most from his stay in prison.
That's easy, he said.
Everything.

MAN OF THE HOUSE *Bob Hicok*

· ·

It was a misunderstanding.
I got into bed, made love
with the woman I found there,
called her honey, mowed the lawn,
had three children, painted
the house twice, fixed the furnace,
overcame an addiction to blue pills,
read Spinoza every night
without once meeting his God,
buried one child, ate my share
of Jell-o and meatloaf,
went away for nine hours a day
and came home hoarding my silence,
built a ferris wheel in my mind,
bolt by bolt, then broke it
just as it spun me to the top.
Turns out I live next door.

SONG AGAINST NATURAL SELECTION *Edward Hirsch*

The weak survive!
A man with a damaged arm,
a house missing a single brick, one step
torn away from the other steps
the way I was once torn away
from you; this hurts us, it

isn't what we'd imagined, what
we'd hoped for when we were young
and still hoping for, still imagining things,
but we manage, we survive. Sure,
losing is hard work, one limb severed
at a time makes it that much harder

to get around the city, another word
dropped from our vocabularies
and the remaining words are that much heavier
on our tongues; that much further
from ourselves, and yet people
go on talking, speech survives.

It isn't easy giving up limbs,
trying to manage with that much
less to eat each week, that much more
money we know we'll never make,
things we not only can't buy, but
can't afford to look at in the stores;

this hurts us, and yet we manage, we survive
so that losing itself becomes a kind
of song, our song, our only witness
to the way we die, one day at a time;
a leg severed, a word buried; this
is how we recognize ourselves, and why.

FOR THE SLEEPWALKERS *Edward Hirsch*

Tonight I want to say something wonderful
for the sleepwalkers, who have so much faith
in their legs, so much faith in the invisible

arrow carved into the carpet, the worn path
that leads to the stairs instead of the window,
the gaping doorway instead of the seamless mirror.

I love the way that sleepwalkers are willing
to step out of their bodies into the night,
to raise their arms and welcome the darkness,

palming the blank spaces, touching everything.
Always they return home safely, like blind men
who know it is morning by feeling shadows.

And always they wake up as themselves again.
That's why I want to say something astonishing
like: *Our hearts are leaving our bodies.*

Our hearts are thirsty black handkerchiefs
flying through the trees at night, soaking up
the darkest beams of moonlight, the music

of owls, the motion of wind-torn branches.
And now our hearts are thick black fists
flying back to the glove of our chests.

We have to learn to trust our hearts like that.
We have to learn the desperate faith of sleep-
walkers who rise out of their calm beds

and walk through the skin of another life.
We have to drink the stupefying cup of darkness
and wake up to ourselves, nourished and surprised.

OH MERCY *Tony Hoagland*

Only the millionth person
to glance up at the moon tonight
which looks bald, high-browed and professorial to me,

the kind of face I always shook my fist at
when its back was turned,
when I was seventeen

and every stopsign was a figure of authority
that had it in for me,
and every bottle of cold beer

had a little picture of my father on the label
for smashing down in parking lots
at 2 A.M., when things devolved

into the dance of who was craziest.
That year, if we could have reached the moon,
if we could have shoplifted the paint and telescoping ladders,

we would have scribbled FUCK YOU
upon its massive yellow cheek,
thrilled about the opportunity

to offend three billion people
in a single night.
But the moon stayed out of reach,

imperturbable, polite.
It kept on varnishing the seas,
overseeing the development of grapes in Italy,

putting the midwest to bed
in white pajamas.
It's seen my kind

a million times before
upon this parapet of loneliness and fear
and how we come around in time

to lifting up our heads,
looking for the kindness
that would make revenge unnecessary.

MY COUNTRY *Tony Hoagland*

When I think of what I know about America,
I think of kissing my best friend's wife
in the parking lot of the zoo one afternoon,

just over the wall from the lion's cage.
One minute making small talk, the next
my face was moving down to meet her

wet and open, upturned mouth. It was a kind of patriotic act,
pledging our allegiance to the pleasure
and not the consequence, crossing over the border

of what we were supposed to do,
burning our bridges and making our bed
to an orchestra of screaming birds

and the smell of elephant manure. Over her shoulder
I could see the sun, burning palely in the winter sky
and I thought of my friend, who always tries

to see the good in situations—how an innocence
like that shouldn't be betrayed.
Then she took my lower lip between her teeth,

I slipped my hand inside her shirt and felt
my principles blinking out behind me,
like streetlights in a town where I had never

lived, to which I never intended to return.
And who was left to speak of what had happened?
And who would ever be brave, or lonely,

or free enough to ask?

LAWRENCE *Tony Hoagland*

On two occasions in the past twelve months
I have failed, when someone at a party
spoke of him with a dismissive scorn,
to stand up for D. H. Lawrence,

a man who burned like an acetylene torch
from one end to the other of his life.
These individuals, whose relationship to literature
is approximately that of a tree shredder

to stands of old-growth forest,
these people leaned back in their chairs,
bellies full of dry white wine and the ova of some foreign fish,
and casually dropped his name

the way that pygmies with their little poison spears
strut around the carcass of a fallen elephant.
"O Elephant," they say,
"you are not so big and brave today!"

It's a bad day when people speak of their superiors
with a contempt they haven't earned,
and it's a sorry thing when certain other people

don't defend the great dead ones
who have opened up the world before them.
And though, in the catalogue of my betrayals,
this is a fairly minor entry,

I resolve, if the occasion should recur,
to uncheck my tongue and say, "I love the spectacle
of maggots condescending to a corpse,"
or, "You should be so lucky in your brainy, bloodless life

as to deserve to lift
just one of D. H. Lawrence's urine samples
to your arid psychobiographic
theory-tainted lips."

Or maybe I'll just take the shortcut
between the spirit and the flesh,
and punch someone in the face,
because human beings haven't come that far

in their effort to subdue the body,
and we still walk around like zombies
in our dying, burning world,
able to do little more

than fight, and fuck, and crow:
something Lawrence wrote about
in such a manner
as to make us seem magnificent.

THE COLLABORATION *Tony Hoagland*

That was the summer I used *The Duino Elegies*
in all of my seductions,
taking Rilke from my briefcase

the way another man might break out
candlelight and wine.
I think Rilke would have understood,

would have thought the means
justified the end, as I began to read
in a voice so low it forced my audience

to lean a little closer,
as if Rilke were a limestone bench
stationed on a hillside

where lovers gathered to enjoy the vista
of each other listening.
What a chaperone,

and what a view—is it Susan
I am thinking of?—
how, in the middle of the great *Ninth Elegy*,

in the passage where the poet
promises to memorize the earth,
her tanned and naked knee

seemed the perfect landing platform
for any angels in the vicinity.
I think Rilke would have seen

the outline of an angel
in the space between our bodies
just before we kissed,

then seen it vanish
as we clashed together
and commenced our collaboration

on another chapter
of the famous, familiar and amusing
saga of human relations—choosing

heat instead of grace,
possession over possibility—trading
the kingdom of heaven

one more time
for two arms full
of beautiful, confusing earth.

THE KISS *Paul Hoover*

She had imagined the kiss,
how it would be to have another person
stuck to the edge of her face.
The food at dinner was arranged in a question.
But the kiss itself was awkward.
His glasses were smashed between them,
and both of their noses were crooked.
She thought he was looking over her shoulder
into some void or other,
but he was thinking of the cure for baldness,
a bottle of which he had in his pocket,
making a bulge between them.
When they withdrew from the kiss,
she saw his rolled-up eyes,
the kind you see on statues,
and thought, "He don't look so hot."
But then they kissed at her mother's grave
and beneath the painting of an Aztec warrior
holding his naked bride.
They kissed on a cliff overlooking the edge of the world
and in a parking lot where the smell of fish and rot
barely disturbed their ardor.
They kissed in an elevator,
both rising and falling,
and at the bowling alley,
as if upon a stage.
Then they kissed in a rattle or survey of swans—
whatever you call such a thing.
The curious birds ran their necks
up the legs of his pants
and also beneath her skirt.
Naturally, this was the best kiss ever,
and they were crazy in love.

SWEEP *Rodney Jones*

The two Garnett brothers who run the Shell station here,
who are working separately just now,
one hunched under the rear axle of Skippy Smith's Peterbilt tractor,
the other humming as he loosens the clamps
to replace my ruptured heater hoses,
have aged twenty years since I saw them last
and want only to talk of high school
and who has died from each class.
Seamless gray sky, horns from the four-lane,
the lot's oil slicks rainbowing and dimpling with rain.
I have been home for three days, listening to an obituary.
The names of relatives met once,
of men from the plant where he works,
click like distant locks on my father's lips.
I know that it is death that obsesses him
more than football or weather
and that cancer is far too prevalent
in this green valley of herbicides and chemical factories.
Now Mike, the younger brother,
lifts from my engine compartment
a cluster of ruined hoses,
twisted and curled together like a nest of blacksnakes,
and whistles as he forages in the rack
for more. Slowly, the way things work down here,
while I wait and the rain plinks on the rims of overturned tires,
he and my father trade the names of the dead:
Bill Farrell for Albert Dotson,
Myles Hammond, the quick tackle of our football team,
for Don Appleton, the slow, redheaded one.
By the time the rack is exhausted
I'm thinking if I lived here all year I'd buy American,
I'd drive a truck, and I'm thinking
of football and my father's and Mike's words
staking out an absence I know I won't reclaim.
Because I don't get home much anymore,
I notice the smallest scintilla of change,
every burnt-out trailer and newly paved road,
and the larger, slower change

that is exponential,
that strangeness, like the unanticipated face
of my aunt, shrunken and perversely stylish
under the turban she wore after chemotherapy.
But mostly it's the wait, one wait after another,
and I'm dropping back deep in the secondary
under the chill and pipe smoke of a canceled October
while the sweep rolls toward me from the line of scrimmage,
and Myles Hammond, who will think too slowly
and turn his air-force jet into the Arizona desert,
and Don Appleton, who will drive out on a country road
for a shotgun in his mouth, are cut down,
and I'm shifting on the balls of my feet,
bobbing and saving one nearly hopeless feint,
one last plunge for the blockers
and the ballcarrier who follows the sweep,
and it comes, and comes on.

TRAITOR *Allison Joseph*

What did that girl on the playground mean
when she hissed *you ain't black* at me,

pigtails bouncing, her hands
on her bony hips? She sucked her teeth,

stared at me with such contempt
that I wanted to hide in my mother's

skirts, wanted to scurry to my house's
hall closet, safe among the great

dark coats. *You talk funny*, she said,
all proper, as if pronunciation

was a sin, a scandal, a strike
against the race only a traitor

would perform, an Uncle Tom sellout.
Somehow I'd let her down by not

slurring, I'd failed her by not
letting language laze on its own,

its sound unhurried. I'd said
isn't rather than *ain't*,

called my mother *mom* instead
of *momma*, pronounced *th* distinctly

so no one would confuse *them*
with *dem, those* with *dose.*

Your momma talk that funny?
the girl demanded, her face

in my face now, her nose
inches from mine, her eyes

lit by something near hate,
but more ferocious, a kind

of disgust mixed with pity,
disdain. *We're from Canada,*

I said, and the girl's eyes
went wide, as if I'd said

cantaloupe, or *harpoon,*
or some nonsense word like

*abracadabra. There must not be
no black folks in Canada then,*

she sneered, leaning in further,
pushing on my chest with one

bony finger, pinning me there
like a bug to a fly screen,

pressing me so hard that
my lower lip started to tremble

on its own, a sign of weakness
she laughed a mocking, heavy

laugh at, telling me *go on and cry,
white girl, cry till your momma*

can hear, pushing me so I toppled
onto my back, ripping the pants

my mother warned me not to rip.
She stood over me, laughing

like she'd just seen the world's
best clown, laughing though I

was just as dark as she,
my hair in the same

nappy plaits, my skin
the same rough brown.

GOOD HUMOR *Allison Joseph*

In our neighborhood of run-down houses,
of abandoned lots and corner groceries,
nothing tasted better than ice cream's

sweet delight: the delicate peaks
and swirls of vanilla soft-serve,
cold chill of Italian ices

scraped from their containers
with tiny wooden spoons—cherry
and rainbow staining teeth, gums.

How we loved orange push-ups
that melted down our fingers,
so sticky we couldn't help

licking our thumbs and fingertips,
palms grasping at the slippery
treats. Remember the red, white

and blue bomb pops, sugar
and color frozen on a stick,
popsicles almost too heavy

to handle, almost too large
for the child-mouths that
welcomed them, sucking until

the colors faded, until
pallid ice was left behind.
All the flavors we could want

lived in the white truck
that cruised our streets
on summer afternoons: coconut

and chocolate, strawberry shortcake
and lemon-lime, peach and succulent
pineapple pulling us through

those heavily humid summer days.
We'd listen for the faint music
of that truck, wrangle dollars

and quarters from parents,
grandparents, and line up,
one behind the other, ready

to cool our tongues, freeze our teeth,
longing to lick and swallow everything
that melted beneath the summer sun.

SOUL TRAIN *Allison Joseph*

Oh how I wanted to be a dancer
those Saturday mornings in the
living room, neglecting chores

to gape at the whirling people
on our television: the shapely
and self-knowing brownskinned

women who dared stare straight
at the camera, the men strong,
athletically gifted as they

leaped, landed in full splits.
No black people I knew lived
like this—dressed in sequins,

make-up, men's hair slicked
back like 40s gangsters,
women in skin-tight, merciless

spandex, daring heels higher
than I could imagine walking in,
much less dancing. And that

dancing!—full of sex, swagger,
life—a communal rite where
everyone arched, swayed, shimmered

and shimmied, hands overhead
in celebration, bodies moving
to their own influences, lithe

under music pumping from studio
speakers, beneath the neon letters
that spelled out SOUL TRAIN—

the hippest trip in America.
I'd try to dance, to keep up,
moving like the figures on

the screen, hoping the rhythm
could hit me in that same
hard way, that same mission

of shake and groove, leaving
my dust rag behind, ignoring
the furniture and the polish

to step and turn as they did,
my approximation nowhere near
as clever or seductive, faking

it as best I knew how, shaking
my 12-year-old self as if something
deep depended upon the right move,

the righteous step, the insistent
groove I followed, yearning to get
it right, to move like those dancers—

blessed by funk, touched with rhythm,
confident in their motions, clothes,
their spinning and experienced bodies.

THE CHILDREN'S BOOK OF
KNOWLEDGE *Jesse Lee Kercheval*

· ·

The horse stands near a well whose rim is the edge of the world.
Inside, lives only the Frog King, voice a fat old cello. We are not
tall, sister, you and I, but we stand in the center of the barnyard,
prayed over by the rooster's red and dusty wings. In this picture,
moon and sun together light our way home to a supper of bread and
jam, sweet and milky tea. This is the time before large, before time
began to click faster and faster. Before we learned to talk and kept
talking, learned to read, no book answering the question—*Why this
life?* Before our childhood, like a moth, closed its velvet wings.

YOUR WIFE, A WIDOW, WAITS FOR YOU *Jesse Lee Kercheval*

You have bicycled off a cliff,
ridden onto the lake
where the ice is rotten.
You are falling,
your green Schwinn caught
under buses, tractors,
a Presidential motorcade.
You are an hour late.

When I bought the bike
for your birthday,
I walked it home.
How could I let you
ride unguarded
through the air
with only faith
between you and the asphalt?

I close my eyes and dream
you trapped and then
untrap you. I dream
you hurt and heal you.
I multiply you until
when you come whirring
through the gate,
you are followed by yourself
and yourself and yourself.
Extra husbands, just in case.

THINGS THAT HAVE ESCAPED ME *Jesse Lee Kercheval*

A blue parakeet named Julie
we bought at Woolworth's.
My mother said she flew out
the open kitchen window
while I was at nursery school.
For weeks, I looked
in every tree,
Julie Julie Julie,
sure she would starve
without her birdseed bell.
No, my mother said,
someone else will find her,
give her a good home.

A guinea pig named Grumpy
on a weekend pass
from kindergarten.
I left him in my doll carriage,
went to eat my dinner.
He chewed through the plastic cloth,
fled into the ductwork.
That winter, before they turned
the heat on, my parents
sold the house. Maybe
because of Grumpy,
maybe not.

Now it is my daughter
who pets a guinea pig.
This time at the zoo
where there are more
exotic animals,
but not ones she can touch.
He is talking to me,
she says, sure as any human
that the animals we keep
behind bars or locked
apartment doors

care for us
above all other humans,
above their own kind.
Her pig does gaze up
at her, fur ruffled,
brown eyes fixed.

I will get you out of here,
she whispers
in his furry ear.
Maybe she is right,
maybe this time
child and pet escape together.
She fits him
with her own small coat
and they slip past
the zoo guards
quite unnoticed.
Just a pretty blond girl
and her ugly sharp-toothed
baby brother.

Or maybe it is only
my daughter escaping,
from the zoo, from me.
Speeding through time
a baby, a toddler,
now a woman driving
to Kansas City
for an interview
with Hallmark.
Mom on the lawn, waving—
Write when you get work!
Knowing at the most
she will get a card.

I lied, my mother said
years later,
about your parakeet.
I found her on the bottom
of her cage.

Feet up, eyes closed.
I wanted you to think
she'd gone on to better things.
I sat unbelieving,
How could you be sure
that she was dead?
Remember, my mother said,
the turtle we bought,
the goldfish?
That bird was dead.
She didn't escape
any more than they did,
any more than I will.

Unless, she said,
death is escape.
My mother in the hospital,
crying—*Get me out of here.*
God or someone answering.
My father on the telephone to me,
having his last heart attack
long distance. In the end,
what does not escape us?
Pets, parents, children,
all the plans we make,
unmake. Time, our lives,
the very molecules
we're made of.
The universe
is racing from us
at the speed of light
and it is never
coming back.

ACCEPTANCE SPEECH *Elizabeth Kerlikowske*

What can I do when I hate my city, Kalamazoo?
When I am pacing at my window staring out
hating the porch drunks
hating the parentless children looking for direction
hating the cruising teens
the sexy bleached young punked-out beater hoods
I can't control the dribbling of the midnight ball
or the barking of the backyard dogs at squirrels
anymore than I can control the flowering of the catalpa
late in May
I must stop fighting what I can't control
I must instead accept
I accept that I need to accept
My acceptance starts here
I accept Kalamazoo for its sins and its mellifluous name
I accept the city sounds of rough tumblehousing ball
in the twilight under budding oaks
I accept city studs sweltering on street corners
hailing cars with crack and bullets
I accept you crack dealers
you Detroit boys with your wayward plastic shower caps
and Cadillacs
your short sad lives
I accept you as I accept dogs running through my garden
not maliciously but because it has become dog nature
I accept cats screaming for LUV in the night
I accept the strangers who've chosen Egleston Avenue
as the stage for their domestic drama
I applaud them and the cruiser which removes them
as excellent ticketless theater
I accept the Roman Candle
which interrupts the boring rut of my sleep
I accept your muffler sparking along the street
I know if you could you would have a new car
I accept food stamps
and people with more than ten items
in the Express Lane at Town and Country

and I accept you
I accept your singing, your dancing, your
salsa, your rap, your Roger Whitaker
I accept cultural diversity
but I will not accept imitations
I accept the Milwood Little League, the Girl Scouts
the Boys and Girls Clubs selling candy bars all in the same week
the week I begin my diet
I accept you, Jehovah's Witness, and I accept your *Watch Tower*
but only because I recycle
I accept the pest controllers in their unmarked cars
for the neighbors' sake
I accept that children must explore
and that woods in the city are more fictive than fact
I accept that boys throw things
that potholes are born one moment before
I drive where they just weren't
and that cotton clothing shrinks as I age
I accept that reluctantly
I let the thirsty postman in for water
My children leave him Easter candy melting in the mailbox
and he accepts it and even flirts with me
What a city!
I accept my paycheck from Western Michigan University
I accept my trees being axed for the convenience
of Consumer's Power but not without a fight
I accept my city with a grain of salt because I don't want a goiter
I accept my limitations as a WASP human in a darkening world
I accept the Eurocentric fountain in Bronson Park
because I know now the Indians were here all along
and Columbus discovered not America but his own limitations
I accept and revere the Rex Cafe, the Mermaid Lounge, the State
Theater, Washington Square Library, the Gilmore drive,
the Upjohn money
I accept the pill smell that sometimes hangs
over the Edison Neighborhood
I accept that our groundwater is unacceptable
and I fight for change
I accept the formations of geese and Blue Angels in the June sky
I accept Kalamazoo from Ada Street to Bronson Boulevard
because it's not Heaven or Hell or Grand Rapids

Kalamazoo is like the birthmark on my forehead
I hated until I was told
"Have it removed" and I couldn't
Unthinkable
It belonged there as I belong here
I accepted that and Kalamazoo
I accept you

I THINK I AM GOING TO CALL MY
WIFE PARAGUAY *David Kirby*

I think I am going to call my wife Paraguay,
for she is truly bilingual,
even though she speaks no Guaraní
and, except for "cucaracha" and "taco,"
hardly any Spanish at all.
She has two zones, though,
one a forest luxuriant with orchids
and the smell of fruit trees,
where the Indians worship
the pure and formless Tupang,
who shines in the lightning
and roars in the thunder,
the other a dry plain,
a flat place with the soul of a mountain,
motionless and hard as a rock.
During the day the sun blazes
on the red dust of Paraguay
as dark-eyed, straight-backed women
walk home from the river
with bundles of laundry on their heads,
hoping to avoid trouble,
for the Paraguayans are always fighting;
young conscripts lolling in faded cotton uniforms
have no idea whether they will be summoned next
to overthrow the government or defend it.
My wife Paraguay and I
ourselves had to fight the War of the Triple Alliance,
although in our case
it wasn't Brazil, Uruguay, and Argentina
but Harry, Edward, and Maurice,
her former boyfriends. I won.
War does not silence Paraguay
or dismay her in any way,
for still her people shout on the football fields
and whisper declarations of love
on the darkened patios of the old colonial houses,

just as my wife Paraguay says that she loves me
as the parroquet and toucan fly over
and the perfume of the lime and orange tree
blow through the windows of our big house,
which I call South America
because it contains Paraguay
and is shaped like a sweet potato.

AMAZED BY CHEKHOV *David Kirby*

. . . .

Whenever I see a production
of *Wild Honey*, say, or *The Seagull,*
I want to run up on stage
and drink vodka with the characters I admire
and knock the villains down
and have all the women throw themselves at my feet.
I forget that the people up there
are just actors who would probably freeze
or hurry off as the curtain came down
and that I would be hustled away by understudies,
eager nobodies destined for nothing better
than television commercials, if they're lucky,
but trying now to impress the stars
by the force with which they hurl me into the alley,
where I bruise and cut myself and tear my clothes.
As for my wife, well!
There would be a study in anger for you!
"You've embarrassed me for the last time,"
she'd say, and that would be the end of,
not a perfect marriage, but a good one nonetheless.
On the other hand, maybe the players would say,
"Marvellous! Wonderful! You're here at last,
old man! Have a drink!"
                              And that would be my life:
I'd spend the rest of my days acting my heart out
and getting these huge rounds of applause.
I would have to say the same thing over and over again,
but at least it would be brilliant.
And even though something terrible would happen to me
sooner or later, that's simply the price
that would have to be paid by a character
as well-loved as mine. Then *quoi faire?*
as one of Chekhov's impoverished Francophiles would say.
How's this: to get up some evening
when the jokes and the non sequiturs
are flying around like crazy
and make my way to the end of the aisle
as if to go for an ice cream or the bathroom

and get a running start
and fly up the steps
with a big stupid grin on my face
and just disappear into the light.

THE DANCE OF HUSBANDS IN BATHROBES *David Kirby*

From the windows of the house
at the top of the hill
comes a stately music;
it is the funeral lament of Palestrina,
mourning his first wife
now that he is about
to take a second, a wealthy widow.

Men shuffle from doorways
half-asleep; it is the Dance
of Husbands in Bathrobes.
They have something to say
with their slipper-shod feet,
their awkward hands,
unready for the day's work,
their thin, disorderly hair,
but they do not know what it is.

They advance, pick up the morning paper,
turn this way and that.
Wives and children rush to the window
to gasp and applaud
as the husbands leap higher and higher,
dancing and weeping—
the sun is breaking their hearts!
Look, look, they are sinking into
such sorrow as only happy men can know.

NOSEBLEED, GOLD DIGGER, KGB, HENRY JAMES, HANDSHAKE *David Kirby*

Here's the thing: you're coming out of the men's room
and you run into someone you work with and he says

Hi, hows it going and you say Fine, you?
and he says Great and you go to your office

and he goes to the men's room and then
you run into him again on your way back,

only this time you say nothing to him and vice versa.
Is that because you don't have to or because

you don't want to? Nothing has changed
in those few minutes, surely, but perhaps you should ask,

and he should, too, because what if he had a nosebleed
in the men's room and needs to hear you say

That's nothing, happens to me all the time
or Here's the number of a good doctor?

Or say you got the bad phone call from your wife
who says That's it, you creep, I'm out of here,

giving this colleague the chance to say
You can get her back, give her this big ring,

or I always thought she was a cheap gold digger,
better luck next time. We could check on

each other constantly, of course, but that
would lead to crazy stuff, calling up in the middle

of the night to see if the other person is sleeping
or walking in on someone else's big sexy interlude

and saying Whew, you're doing great, thank god.
So let this poem be my signal to each of you

that I am thinking of you all the time;
if you're reading this, I'm looking out for you,

kind of: if you visited Russia in the old days,
the KGB would assign you a "minder" so you wouldn't steal

any state secrets but also to help you
if you get lost, and frankly, I'd rather be lost.

Also, what secret could the state have
that could possibly interest any right-minded person?

Be kind, be kind, be kind, said Henry James,
but that was easy for him to say, since he spent

most of his life alone. Nameless colleague,
I salute you and set down herewith my best wishes

for a *bonne continuation*: I shake your hand!
And you hers, and she his, and so on.

COLORING *Ron Koertge*

. . . .

Here is the handyman with black legs
whistling in spite of gangrene. There
are some smiling cows, red as sores.
A jaundiced mare is chewing peacefully.
Two pea-green farmers chat about nausea.

Cute, but no real grasp of the agricultural
situation. And ending mysteriously
around twelve or thirteen with only
the white crayola intact, used for the silly
sheep, a snowman or the rare Klan meeting.

And no wonder! Whoever heard of The Nobel
Coloring Prize. Who says, "This is my son.
He has a Ph.D. in Coloring." Certainly
no one ever grows up and gets a job in
the Arco Plaza—"The Chairman can't see
you now he's coloring can't see you now
he's in a crayon seminar can't see you
now he's about to do the barn."

Perhaps some gland does it. Subdued by
greasier hormones it atrophies or sleeps
as we crouch at the window on rainy days
every new hair on our new bodies standing
on end as the pillows become the kids at
school we want to kiss or kill as we move out
of childhood outside the lines into
the real where the sun is not a perfect
cookie in the sky but a big hot thing
like us threatening to destroy the world.

ALL SUFFERING COMES FROM ATTACHMENT *Ron Koertge*

—The Buddha

A penis is the ultimate attachment: body's gimmick,
spigot, mitre, millstone around the waist. If it
is huge, who can be sure he is loved for himself
or is it that Washington Monument down there?
If it is small, why was he burdened with so little?
If it is average, is it average enough?

Like any deity, it has a hundred names: some like
a flower (genitalia), aquatic fowl (the dork), part
of a tool kit (whonker). Temperamental and fiery,
the penis is tenor of the body's opera. Inquisitive
and scary, it rises from apparent sleep, a little Lazarus.
Spoiled child, it gets its own way. Or pouts.

As king of matter, it is often the last profound
attachment, the thing that some men cling to—
Oh awful blessing—with both hands.

In the winnowing of parts, the silly feet walk off
alone, muscles of the arms and chest being ornaments
of desire are put away, pretty hair is exorcised by age
or shears. Finally we come to the penis, last wand
in the body's immaculate kingdom.

And if someone can say goodbye to that, to dreams
of himself as father, lover, stallion, warlord,
guy, then the suffering is over at last
and nameless bliss begins.

WHAT SHE WANTED *Ron Koertge*

was my bones. As I gave them
to her one at a time, she put them
in a bag from Saks.

As long as I didn't hesitate
she collected scapula and
vertebrae with a smile.

If I grew reluctant, she pouted.
Then I would come across
with rib cage or pelvis.

Eventually I lay in a puddle
at her feet, only the boneless
penis waving like an anemone.

"Look at yourself," she said.
"You're disgusting."

FOOLISH EARTHLINGS *Ron Koertge*

That's what they call us, those icky guys
from somewhere out there with their syrupy
heads or tin lips. And right after we've
welcomed them with open arms and let
them take our homecoming queen and her
first runner-up on a tour of the saucer's
medical facilities.

No wonder the dorky scientist is ticked off.
No wonder he and the trim first lieutenant
work so hard to find a chink in the DNA.
And naturally they succeed and just in time.
So the fiends from Cygnus lose again.

Here's some advice for spacemen. Take it
easy with the scorn. Learn a couple of jokes,
buy a round when it's your turn, keep your
eyes (all your eyes, pal) off our daughters.
Say, "We come in peace." Say it a lot.
We're suckers for that.

THE SEVEN DWARFS, EACH ON HIS DEATHBED, REMEMBER SNOW WHITE *Ron Koertge*

Sleepy: I wanted to get her into the feathers alright,
          but just to snooze. I tried to make her under-
          stand that, but oh no. Always the raised eye-
          brow and wagging finger.

Dopey: When she turned up, I knew she wouldn't stay.
          When she fell asleep like that, I knew it
          wouldn't last. By acting dopey I got out of
          a lot of work but really I'm sharp as the
          next guy.

Grumpy: Snow White? I barely remember. Besides, what
          did she know about chronic pain. I believe
          she danced, but you couldn't prove it by me.
          Every night I was in bed early, doubled up.

Doc: Snow White worried about her health and about
          getting old. She was tyrannical about physical
          examinations: once a week was nothing. Of
          course a woman her size and complexion was
          exciting, but I soon got used to it.

Bashful: We didn't have a t.v. so the others used to
          turn off the lights and make me blush. She
          could get me beet red, just like that. Or
          at first she could. After a while she had to
          get downright bold. And she liked saying
          those things too. I could tell.

Happy: She made very little difference to me. I was
          always happy. I was then, I still am. Even
          now. I imagine I'm ill. Mentally ill, I mean.

Sneezy: I was the most handsome of us all, less
            gnarled, my limbs in more pleasing proportion.
            But my nose runs constantly and my eyes water.
            She preferred me until I sneezed on her fancy
            dress. Then let me tell you, handsome or not,
            that was that.

DEAR SUPERMAN *Ron Koertge*

I know you think that things
will always be the same: I'll rinse
out your tights, kiss you good-bye
at the window, and every few weeks
get kidnapped by some stellar goons.

But I'm not getting any younger,
and you're not getting any older.
Pretty soon I'll be too frail
to take aloft, and with all those
nick-of-time rescues, you're bound
to pick up somebody more tender
and just as ga-ga as I used to be.
I'd hate her for being 17 and
you for being . . . what, 700?

I can see your sweet face as you read
this, and I know you'd like to siphon
off some strength for me, even if it
meant you could only leap small buildings
at a single bound. But you can't,
and, anyway, would I want to
just stand there while everything
else rushed past?

Take care of yourself and of the world
which is your own true love. One day
soon, as you patrol the curved earth,
that'll be me down there tucked in
for good, being what you'll never be
but still

> Your friend,
> Lois Lane

LURID CONFESSIONS *Steve Kowit*

One fine morning they move in for the pinch
& snap on the cuffs—just like that.
Turns out they've known all about you for years,
have a file the length of a paddy-wagon
with everything—tapes, prints, film . . .
the whole shmear. Don't ask me how but
they've managed to plug a mike into one of your molars
and know every felonious move & transgression
back to the very beginning, with ektachromes
of your least indiscretion & pecadillo.
Needless to say, you are thrilled,
tho sitting there in the docket
you bogart it, tough as an old tooth—
your jaw set, your sleeves rolled
& three days of stubble . . . Only,
when they play it back it looks different:
a life common & loathsome as gum stuck to a chair.
Tedious hours of you picking your nose,
scratching, eating, clipping your toenails . . .
Alone, you look stupid; in public, your rapier
wit is slimy & limp as an old bandaid.
They have thousands of pictures of people around you
stifling yawns. As for sex—a bit
of pathetic groping among the unlovely & luckless:
a dance with everyone making steamy love in the dark
& you alone in a corner eating a pretzel.
You leap to your feet protesting
that's not how it was, they have it all wrong.
But nobody hears you. The bailiff
is snoring, the judge is cleaning his teeth,
the jurors are all wearing glasses with eyes painted open.
The flies have folded their wings and stopped buzzing.
In the end, after huge doses of coffee,
the jury is polled. One after another
they manage to rise to their feet
like narcoleptics in August, sealing your fate:
Innocent . . . innocent . . . innocent . . . Right down the line.
You are carried out screaming.

I ATTEND A POETRY READING *Steve Kowit*

The fellow reading poetry at us wouldn't stop.
Nothing would dissuade him:
not the stifling heat; the smoky walls
with their illuminated clocks;
our host, who shifted anxiously
from foot to foot.
Polite applause had stiffened
to an icy silence:
no one clapped
or nodded.
No one sighed.
Surely he must understand that we had families
waiting for us, jobs
we had to get to in the morning.
That chair was murdering my back.
The cappuccino
tasted unaccountably of uric acid.
Lurid bullfight posters flickered
in the red fluorescent light—
& suddenly I knew that I had died,
& for those much too windy readings of my own
had been condemned
to sit forever in this damned cafe.
A squadron of enormous flies
buzzed around the cup of piss
I had been drinking from.
Up at the mike, our poet of the evening
grinned,
& flicked his tail,
& kept on reading.

HELL *Steve Kowit*

I died & went to Hell & it was nothing like L.A.
The air all shimmering & blue. No windows
busted, gutted walk-ups, muggings, rapes.
No drooling hoodlums hulking in the doorways.
Hell isn't anything like Ethiopia or Bangladesh or Bogota:
beggars are unheard of. No one's starving. Nobody
lies moaning in the streets. Nor is it Dachau
with its ovens, Troy in flames, some slaughterhouse
where screaming animals, hung upside down, are bled & skinned.
No plague-infested Avignon or post-annihilation Hiroshima.
Quite the contrary: in Hell everybody's health is fine
forever, & the weather is superb—eternal spring.
The countryside all wildflowers & the cities
hum with commerce: cargo ships bring all the latest
in appliances, home entertainment, foreign culture, silks.
Folks fall in love, have children. There is sex
& romance for the asking. In a word, the place is perfect.
Only, unlike heaven, where when it rains
the people are content to let it rain,
in Hell they live like we do—endlessly complaining.
Nothing as it is is ever right. The astroturf
a nuisance, neighbors' kids too noisy, traffic
nothing but a headache. If the patio were just
a little larger, or the sun-roof on the Winnebago worked.
If only we had darker eyes or softer skin or longer legs,
lived elsewhere, plied a different trade, were slender,
sexy, wealthy, younger, famous, loved, athletic.
Friend, I swear to you as one who has returned
if only to bear witness: no satanic furies
beat their kited wings. No bats shriek overhead.
There are no flames. No vats of boiling oil
wait to greet us in that doleful kingdom.
Nothing of the sort. The gentleman who'll ferry you across
is all solicitude & courtesy. The river black but calm.
The crossing less eventful than one might have guessed.
Though no doubt you will think it's far too windy on the water.
That the glare is awful. That you're tired, hungry, ill
at ease, or that, if nothing else, the quiet is unnerving.
That you need a drink, a cigarette, a cup of coffee.

A TRICK *Steve Kowit*

. . . .

Late afternoon. Huancayo. We'd made the long haul down
from Ayacucho that morning. Were hungry & tired.
Had stumbled into one of those huge, operatic, down-at-the-heels
Peruvian restaurants: red cloths on the tables, teardrop
chandeliers, candles in ribbed silver cages.
Its back wall the remains of an ancient Quechua temple:
that massive, mortarless, perfectly fitted hand-hewn stone
whose secret had died with the Incas.
The place was deserted, except for a middle-aged waiter
tricked out in the shabby black & white jacket
& slacks of the trade. He brought us two menus,
two goblets for wine, a plate of *papas a la huancaina.*
I was unaccountably happy. In one of those giddy,
insouciant moods that come out of nowhere.
The previous summer I'd given the army the slip,
leaving to better men than myself the task of carpet-bombing
the indigent peasants of Asia.
Mary & I had exchanged matrimonial vows in Seattle
& then headed south. Had been bussing for months
from town to town thru the Andes.
The truth is, the whole thing had happened by magic.
                                        "Hey,
you know that trick where you blow an invisible coin
into a sealed-up glass?" I lowered a saucer over her long-
stemmed goblet so nothing could enter, & grinned
as if I knew how to pluck out of nowhere fishes & loaves.
Mary said No, she didn't—& laughed,
preparing herself for another fine piece of buffoonery.
On the table between us, though it wasn't yet dark,
the candle was already lit. In the distance, the misty sierra.
I asked her to hand me a coin, placed it into my palm,
recited some hocus-pocus known only to shamans from Brooklyn,
then spread out my fingers—& lo & behold, it had vanished!
So far so good. But that part was easy. What I did next
was harder—to blow the invisible coin into that covered-up glass.
The nice thing was you could see it fall in with a clatter,
hear the luxurious clink of silver in glass as it dropped
out of nowhere & settled. Needless to say, she was amazed.

195

I mean *really* amazed! & so too was our waiter
who, as it turns out, had been watching the whole affair
from the wall by the kitchen, & flew to my side
flailing his arms like a sinner whose soul the Holy
Spirit had entered, & who knows he is saved.
He wanted to know how I'd done it. How such a thing
could possibly happen. *Milagro*! I felt like Jesus
raising the dead: a little embarrassed, but pleased
that I'd brought the thing off—& that someone had seen it.
Huancayo. I liked the looks of the place: that sharp
mountain light before dusk, folks walking around
on the other side of the window in woolen serapes.
If it wouldn't have sounded so pious
or grandiose, I'd have said to that fellow: "Friend,
how I did it isn't really the point; in this world nothing
is more or less marvelous than anything else."
But I didn't. Instead, I just shrugged, the way
that when Lazarus opened his eyes & shook off the dust
& put on his hat, Jesus himself must have shrugged,
as much as to say it was nothing, a trifle. & that done,
we checked out the menus, & taking our new friend's advice
ordered a huge vegetarian feast—me & Mary, my wife,
that woman who one day—all wit & forbearance
& grace—had fallen, by some sort of miracle, into my life.

THE LAUNDROMAT *Dorianne Laux*

My clothes somersault in the dryer. At thirty
I float in and out of a new kind of horniness,
the kind where you get off on words and gestures;
long talks about art are foreplay, the climax
is watching a man eat a Napoleon while he drives.
Across from me a fifty-year-old matron folds clothes,
her eyes focused on the nipples of a young man in
silk jogging shorts. He looks up, catching her.
She giggles and blurts out, "Hot, isn't it?"
A man on my right eyes the line of my shorts, waiting
for me to bend over. I do. An act of animal kindness.
A long black jogger swings in off the street to
splash his face in the sink and I watch the room
become a sweet humid jungle. We crowd around
the Amazon at the watering hole, twitching our noses
like wildebeests or buffalo, snorting, rooting out
mates in the heat. I want to hump every moving thing
in this place. I want to lie down in the dry dung
and dust and twist to scratch my back. I want to
stretch and prowl and grow lazy in the shade. I want
to have a slew of cubs. "Do you have change for
a quarter?" he asks, scratching the inside of his thigh.
Back in the laundromat my socks are sticking to my
sheets. Caught in the crackle of static electricity,
I fold my underwear. I notice the honey-colored
stains in each silk crotch. Odd-shaped, like dreams,
I make my panties into neat squares and drop them,
smiling, into the wicker basket.

DUST *Dorianne Laux*

Someone spoke to me last night,
told me the truth. Just a few words,
but I recognized it.
I knew I should make myself get up,
write it down, but it was late,
and I was exhausted from working
all day in the garden, moving rocks.
Now, I remember only the flavor—
not like food, sweet or sharp.
More like a fine powder, like dust.
And I wasn't elated or frightened,
but simply rapt, aware.
That's how it is sometimes—
God comes to your window,
all bright light and black wings,
and you're just too tired to open it.

FAST GAS *Dorianne Laux*

. . . .

—For Richard

Before the days of self service,
when you never had to pump your own gas,
I was the one who did it for you, the girl
who stepped out at the sound of a bell
with a blue rag in my hand, my hair pulled back
in a straight, unlovely ponytail.
This was before automatic shut-offs
and vapor seals, and once, while filling a tank,
I hit a bubble of trapped air and the gas
backed up, came arcing out of the hole
in a bright gold wave and soaked me—face, breasts,
belly and legs. And I had to hurry
back to the booth, the small employee bathroom
with the broken lock, to change my uniform,
peel the gas-soaked cloth from my skin
and wash myself in the sink.
Light-headed, scrubbed raw, I felt
pure and amazed—the way the amber gas
glazed my flesh, the searing,
subterranean pain of it, how my skin
shimmered and ached, glowed
like rainbowed oil on the pavement.
I was twenty. In a few weeks I would fall,
for the first time, in love, that man waiting
patiently in my future like a red leaf
on the sidewalk, the kind of beauty
that asks to be noticed. How was I to know
it would begin this way: every cell of my body
burning with a dangerous beauty, the air around me
a nimbus of light that would carry me
through the days, how when he found me,
weeks later, he would find me like that,
an ordinary woman who could rise
in flame, all he would have to do
is come close and touch me.

2 A.M. *Dorianne Laux*

When I came with you that first time
on the floor of your office, the dirty carpet
under my back, the heel of one foot
propped on your shoulder, I went ahead
and screamed, full-throated, as loud
and as long as my body demanded,
because somewhere, in the back of my mind,
packed in the smallest neurons still capable
of thought, I remembered
we were in a warehouse district
and that no sentient being resided for miles.
Afterwards, when I could unclench
my hands and open my eyes, I looked up.
You were on your knees, your arms
stranded at your sides, so still—
the light from the crooknecked lamp
sculpting each lift and delicate twist,
the lax muscles, the smallest veins
on the backs of your hands. I saw
the ridge of each rib, the blue hollow
pulsing at your throat, all the colors
in your long blunt-cut hair which hung
over your face like a raffia curtain
in some south sea island hut.
And as each bright synapse unfurled
and followed its path, I recalled
a story I'd read that explained why women
cry out when they come—that it's
the call of the conqueror, a siren howl
of possession. So I looked again
and it felt true, your whole body
seemed defeated, owned, having taken on
the aspect of a slave in shackles, the wrists
loosely bound with invisible rope.
And when you finally spoke you didn't
lift your head but simply moaned the word *god*

on an exhalation of breath—I knew then
I must be merciful, benevolent,
impossibly kind.

TRACY AND JOE *Lisa Lewis*

You don't want to know how quiet my life's become
That last night when I heard someone scream *Whore*!
It was one in the morning and I was so bored
With black-and-white sitcoms on the all-night station
I hit the mute button on the remote control,
Sidled to the window, and parted the curtains
Just a slice so no one would see me but I could watch
What was going on and do something about it
If it came to that—call the cops, step outside and hope
My mere presence would settle the fight, if that's what
It was; and it was, all right. Two young men
Pursued a woman, their silhouettes in streetlight,
Her permed hair. Her red sportscar was parked
Against the curb. "I'm not lying, Joe!" Her voice
Was shaking. "Don't talk down to me!" Joe was
The tall one, in droopy jeans. "Fucking whore!"
Joe shouted, and the short guy, slight, started
Screaming too: "Pussy! Cunt!" Then my own voice:
"Stop fucking with her!" I didn't care if they heard.
I wanted to fight and get it over with. I saw
The woman run to the car. The men turned back
To the little blue house. I flipped the phone book
To the police station number. I closed it back
And poured a drink of water. One-fifteen. I thought
About sleeping. Then I heard they were at it again.
This time I opened my front door, slowly. I saw
The woman fling her car door wide, jump in
Like an arrow drawn to its target, click on the lights
And peel out into the street. Behind her the men
Stood waving their fists. "Whore! Cunt! Pussy!"
Then they lowered their voices. Tracy, they called her.
Called her "whore" again. "Did you fuck her?"
The tall one, Joe, challenged. "No, man, I wouldn't
Do that to you!" the slim one objected. "Have you
Got a cigarette?" Joe handed one over. "You
Wouldn't fuck her if she spread her legs? Could you
Stop? With her laying right there in front of you?"

The short guy tried to change the subject.
"Come on, let's be friends. What are you
Pissed off about? You got your way." He said it
Bitterly. "Stupid girls. They spread their legs
And you put your dick between them!" The night
Was quiet. Every word was clear. It was easy
To understand what he meant. Women spread
Their legs. Men put their dicks between them.
They think they can't stop. That's how it seems.
Maybe they want the stopping to start before
Anything else does. They don't say so. Maybe they
Think they're doing a favor. Maybe they think
There'll be gratitude later. Maybe they feel sorry
For someone lonely. Maybe they want the sense
Of adventure. Maybe they want to be told they're
Good. Maybe they think they love someone.
I watched the young men. They stopped talking.
I wondered where the woman had fled for comfort.
Today a man parked a car I'd never seen in the drive
Of Joe's little house. He stared out the window,
His forehead glowing. Was he one of them?
I couldn't tell. In the hot afternoon I watched
Through the blinds till my vision wavered. Then
The phone rang, a credit card company, and when
I came back the driveway was empty. I hadn't heard
The engine start or a car door slam. It was quiet
Everywhere, a wind sweeping birdsong
Into the empty street. I'm not afraid. But I know
Truth when I hear it. Tracy peeling out
Into the night where now you'd never guess
That drama played here, and I memorized the lines
Like I'd already heard them a thousand times.

BEER *Gerald Locklin*

It takes a lot to get you there, but it won't
    kill you either.

Kids like it. The foam makes a fine mustache.
    When they go to sleep they dream of goofy
    pink dragons and slippery little smiling
    fish.

To the adolescent it is the first taste of the
    earth's bitterness. He has to pretend it gets him high.
    He is afraid it will give him zits, and maybe it will.
    He gives it to his girl and thinks it is because of it
    she gives herself to him.

She doesn't like the taste of it and never will.
    She doesn't have the thirst for it. She
    is afraid it will give her a gut, and
    maybe it will. Eventually she'll be a
    little insulted when it's offered her.
    And probably should be.

But the best of friendships are formed over
    it. It helps men to speak to each other,
    a difficult thing these days. It lets
    men sing without embarrassment of auld
    lang syne and of the sheep that went astray
    somewhere along the line. It goes excellently
    with pool and pickled eggs, beef jerky and
    baseball games. Contrary to popular opinion,
    it is good for the kidneys, affords them exercise.
    It is good for all the appetites.

We all go beyond it; we always come back to it.
    It is the friend who eases us through
    our philosophies. It is the friend we talk
    to about our women, the one who agrees
    with us that they are not all that
    important. It restores our courage in the

face of cowardly sobrieties. It laughs
with us at our most serious poems, weeps
at our pratfalls. It remembers us; it
takes us back.

Finally, this blessed beer, it eases us towards
   sleep.

TAP DANCING LESSONS   *Gerald Locklin*

back in the second grade
my mother had a brainstorm,
she would sturdy up my spindly legs
with dancing lessons at marge miller's studio.

i had my choice of tap or ballet
and instinctively i chose tap,
not so much because I had anything against homosexuality
as that i sensed the rise of ed sullivan, and the whole third world.

i quit dancing two years later
so as not to miss the notre dame broadcasts,
just as many years later i was to be spared a life of shame
when i quit the boy scouts to watch i love lucy.

the funny thing is, my mother's crazy idea worked.
it worked so well that for years i moved around
with the shape of a wigwam, a sort of winnebago teepee—
picture if you can a six-foot dwarf.

only years of lifting weights and drinking beer
have given me any semblance of an upper body,
and even that, like a glacier succumbing to the centuries,
is sloping badly towards the equatorial belt.

still, i was better at it than you might imagine.
mrs. miller once informed my mother that i was
her "little fred astaire." and even now, at parties,
i am apt to break into my "shuffle-off-to-buffalo."

i have two other steps in my repertoire:
the "bell step," although i barely leave the floor now,
and the old standby "stamp-shuffle-ball-change."
the "cossack squat" is just a memory.

THE LEADER OF THE PACK *Gerald Locklin*

in my fantasy i am the leader
of a gang of bikers.

except that we are all middle-aged,
have bad backs, and ride
exercycles in formation.

LEARNING TO SEE CROOKED *Gerald Locklin*

"mommie," she says, "i've never seen you and daddy
kiss."

"Of course you have," the mother says;
"you've just forgotten."

"i wouldn't have forgotten that," she says,
"because i always wish you would."

"it doesn't matter," her father says. "we
both love you and we love each other in our
own way."

"you've seen us kiss," the mother says.

"not on the mouth. not the way people
kiss on your soap operas."

"your mother and i have been together
nearly twenty years," her father says.
"we did a lot of kissing in our time.
that's why we have you and your brother,
thank god."

"maybe you did, but you don't now,"
their daughter says.

the father says, "your mother and i sleep
in the same bed. we do our best to get along
and we have our love for you and your brother
in common. there are things we have come to
understand that you will someday also understand."

this almost satisfies her, but she adds,
"i think you wish that mommie still kissed you."

the mother says, "if you're finished eating,
you may leave the table."

**DO YOU REMEMBER THE SCENE IN *THE GODFATHER*
WHERE JAMES CAAN SAYS, "NOW MAKE SURE THAT THE
GUN GETS STASHED IN THE REST ROOM—I DON'T WANT
MY KID BROTHER WALKING OUT OF THERE WITH
NOTHING BUT HIS DICK IN HIS HAND"?** *Gerald Locklin*

because i knew i would be walking her
through some of the meaner night streets
of downtown l.a., i reached in my glove compartment
and slipped a fold-back knife in my pocket.
and we did run the gamut of some fairly unsavory
concentrations of humanity, but as each potentially
tense encounter approached, i patted my pocket
and felt a little less naked.

safely back in the car
i extracted the weapon from my pocket
and found us both gazing at
a b-flat harmonica accidentally filched,
years ago, from one of fred voss's
dodecaphonic parties.

LETTER TO MY ASSAILANT *Suzanne Lummis*

On such occasions
one comes to know someone spectacularly fast.
Even with your unfriendly arm at my throat
you could hide nothing from me.
Your failures with women, for instance
filed through my mind, failures
moral and physical.
And I knew your father was hostile to doors.
He liked to slam them or break them down.
Your mother worked her whole life
without hoping for anything.
She grew thin. Even in her grave
she kept shrinking. Now she's thin
as a needle, one nearly invisible
hand folded over the other.
I even knew without looking
your socks had red diamonds balanced one
on the other. In fact,
with my breath stopped short in my throat,
your whole life flashed past my eyes,
but I didn't let on.
"I can't breathe," I gasped,
and you loosened your hold. I suppose
I should have been grateful.
Instead I felt impatient with men,
with their small favors.
Perhaps you felt the same about me.
You'd no sooner reached through my torn blouse,
when my scream made you bolt.
We leapt from each other
like two hares released from a trap. Oh oh,
something's not right between men and women.
Perhaps we talked too much,
or did we leave too much unsaid?

For instance, when you ripped my shirt,
mumbling, "I don't want to hurt you,"

I replied, "That's what they all say."
I'll admit I was glib, if you'll admit
you were insensitive. Look,
the world is brimming with happy couples,
benign marriages, with men and women
who've adjusted to each other's defects.
Couldn't we adjust to each other's defects?
I'll begin by trying harder not to forget you,
to remember more clearly
your approximate height, and your brown shirt
which I described to the police.
Our encounter must stand out in our minds,
irrefutable, distinct from all others.
I never intended
all this to become blurred in my memory,
to confuse you with other men.

FISH I REMEMBER *Suzanne Lummis*

Only Birmingham, who took a double back flip
out of his bowl
and flopped till dead on the linoleum.
He looked so alone when I found him,
a spot of gold worth nothing.
He'd wanted to strike out in the world
but couldn't walk or fly or breathe air.
He couldn't trudge ahead
with even the tiniest suitcase.
Birmingham, on our side of the glass
life is that way for us too,
brutal and unjust.
But think of that falling swoop through the air!
Your heart in your mouth,
for an instant you were precious metal, a star.
You were manna dropping from heaven.
You were like the life that burst
in mysterious splendor
long ago from the sea.
I waded,
and tossed him into a wave
at Laguna, with no ceremony.
His little dream went down
into the grey blue.
Mine also. I had to clamber
from the sea as a woman,
not a new thing,
and drive home through the gritty air,
not step from this earth
and soar.

WHY LIFE IS WORTH LIVING *Suzanne Lummis*

. . . .

"One could always say that instead of the hand grasping
the apple the hand thrusts the entire universe backwards,
propelling the apple against the hand."
—The Relativity Explosion

And here you thought you were ineffectual.
At 2:00 A.M. the pipes of your sink
explode, drowning the air.
You rush in. It's as if water
is walking on water.
And every knob you turn lets go
of another geyser.
Then you know water has rebelled against you.
It will never again lie down,
still and serviceable.

And when you wear something new
and quite expensive,
a man attacks you with a glass of wine
then apologizes like mad. He'll turn out to be
some worthless stranger
with whom you'll have an affair.

Then historians will record that on March 3,
P.M., 1979, across the world
all unfaithful husbands left home
for their new loves,
except your man who went back to his wife.

And when you die you'll be boxed
and shipped to the wrong funeral,
to a gathering where you're recognized
and widely disliked.

And yet, on this dusty unkempt planet,
on which felons have urinated,
on which drunks have vomited for countless years,
there is still one last
unimpeachable glory.

See that ungrasped apple on the kitchen counter?
Let your hand reach.
The earth slides backwards, carrying
a myriad of other planets,
and the sparkling darkness between them,
and tiny lenses of stars,
and great unwieldy suns.

Stand still
and give thanks.
All of space, your life,
all that life is
has brought you this gift. It is fruit
crowning your palm like manna
from some better world.

THE PEOPLE OF THE OTHER VILLAGE *Thomas Lux*

hate the people of this village
and would nail our hats
to our heads for refusing in their presence to remove them
or staple our hands to our foreheads
for refusing to salute them
if we did not hurt them first: mail them packages of rats,
mix their flour at night with broken glass.
We do this, they do that.
They peel the larynx from one of our brothers' throats.
We devein one of their sisters.
The quicksand pits they built were good.
Our amputation teams were better.
We trained some birds to steal their wheat.
They sent to us exploding ambassadors of peace.
They do this, we do that.
We canceled our sheep imports.
They no longer bought our blankets.
We mocked their greatest poet
and when that had no effect
we parodied the way they dance
which did cause pain, so they, in turn, said our God
was leprous, hairless.
We do this, they do that.
Ten thousand (10,000) years, ten thousand
(10,000) brutal, beautiful years.

UPON SEEING AN ULTRASOUND PHOTO
OF AN UNBORN CHILD *Thomas Lux*

Tadpole, it's not time yet to nag you
about college (though I have some thoughts
on that), baseball (ditto), or abstract
principles. Enjoy your delicious,
soupy womb-warmth, do some rolls and saults
(it'll be too crowded soon), delight in your early
dreams—which no one will attempt to analyze.
For now: may your toes blossom, your fingers
lengthen, your sexual organs grow (too soon
to tell which yet) sensitive, your teeth
form their buds in their forming jawbone, your already
booming heart expand (literally
now, metaphorically later); O your spine,
eyebrows, nape, knees, fibulae,
lungs, lips . . . But your soul,
dear child: I don't see it here, when
does that come in, whence? Perhaps God,
and your mother, and even I—we'll all contribute
and you'll learn yourself to coax it
from wherever: your soul, which holds your bones
together and lets you live
on earth.—Fingerling, sidecar, nubbin,
I'm waiting, it's me, Dad,
I'm out here. You already know
where Mom is. I'll see you more directly
upon arrival. You'll recognize
me—I'll be the tall-seeming, delighted
blond guy, and I'll have
your nose.

SO YOU PUT THE DOG TO SLEEP *Thomas Lux*

. . . .

"I have no dog, but it must be
Somewhere there's one belongs to me."
—John Kendrick Bangs

You love your dog and carve his steaks
(marbled, tender, aged) in the shape of hearts.
You let him on your lap at will

and call him by a lover's name: Liebchen,
pooch-o-mine, lamby, honey-tart,
and you fill your voice with tenderness, woo.

He loves you too, that's his only job,
it's how he pays his room and board.
Behind his devotion, though, his dopey looks,

might be a beast who wants your house,
your wife; who in fact loathes you, his lord.
His jaws snapping while asleep means dreams

of eating your face: nose, lips, eyebrows, ears . . .
But soon your dog gets old, his legs
go bad, he's nearly blind, you purée his meat

and feed him with a spoon. It's hard to say
who hates whom the most. He will not beg.
So you put the dog to sleep. Bad dog.

MEN WITH SMALL HEADS *Thomas Lux*

and women with small heads
were everywhere
in my hometown when I was six.
Two men standing on the corner: small heads.
Small head: a woman leans to look in her mailbox.
Then there'd be some normal bodies, normal heads.
Not everyone,
in other words, in my hometown
had small heads
but many did, enough
that I'd say to my mother, father: *why*
does that man have a small head?
I was glad my parents'
heads were normal-size.
They were glad I (mostly) didn't ask
why a person with a small head
had a small head
within earshot of that person. Apparently
these small heads
did not appear so small to them.
They had my eyes checked first.
They took some x-rays of my skull.
Did I have migraines?
Did I have pinhead fears, dreams?
Perhaps it was the angle through the windshield glass?
The local Dr. leaning over me
with his penlight probing
my retina—his head was huge
and the hairs on the back of his hand
were crossed like swords. Nothing wrong
with my eyes or my brain
that he could tell
but the heads I swore were small
were not, they were just your average heads,
circa 1953,
just your average heads,
in America.

"I LOVE YOU SWEATHEART"   *Thomas Lux*

A man risked his life to write the words.
A man hung, upsidedown (an idiot friend
holding his legs?) with spraypaint
to write the words on a girder 50 ft. above
a highway. And his beloved,
the next morning driving to work . . . ?

His words are not (meant to be) so unique.
Does she recognize his handwriting?
Did he hint to her at her doorstep the night before
of "something special, darling, tomorrow"?
And did he call her at work
expecting her to faint with delight
at his celebration of her, his passion, his risk?
She will *know* I love her now,
the *world* will know my love for her!
A man risked his life to write the words.
Love is like this at the bone, we hope, love
is like this, Sweatheart, all sore and dumb
and dangerous, ignited, blessed—always,
regardless, no exceptions,
always in blazing matters like these: blessed.

UNCLE EGGPLANT *Jeffrey McDaniel*

· ·

When I was a teenager,
my parents would go away
and stick me with the job
of watching blind Uncle Harry.

I'd buckle him in the front
seat of my Chevy Nova
and take him with me
on drug runs into the city.

Okay, Har, you wait here—
I'm gonna dash into this flower
shop and pick up the azaleas.
One day, I returned to the car,

and Harry was gone. I sped
home, placed an eggplant
on his pillow, and told my
parents *I found him this way.*

THE BAD PILGRIM ROOM *Jeffrey McDaniel*

· ·

When I misbehaved as a child,
my parents would make me undress.
Instead of spanking me,
they'd paint my rear end red,

then place me in a black cloak,
a tall black hat, shoes with buckles,
and lead me down the basement stairs
to the bad pilgrim room.

THE QUIET WORLD *Jeffrey McDaniel*

In an effort to get people to look
into each other's eyes more,
and also to appease the mutes,
the government has decided
to allot each person exactly one hundred
and sixty-seven words, per day.

When the phone rings, I put it to my ear
without saying hello. In the restaurant
I point at chicken noodle soup.
I am adjusting well to the new way.

Late at night, I call my long distance lover,
proudly say *I only used fifty-nine today.*
I saved the rest for you.

When she doesn't respond,
I know she's used up all her words,
so I slowly whisper *I love you*
thirty-two and a third times.
After that, we just sit on the line
and listen to each other breathe.

PLAY IT AGAIN, SALMONELLA *Jeffrey McDaniel*

Watching a man vomit on the sidewalk
is like going back to my alma mater,

where I was voted most likely to secede.

I carried white lies so far they changed
colors. I held tantrums in my pocket

a long time, before I actually threw them.

I was born with dynamite in my chest.
Some days I wish the real me would stand up

and shout *table for ten, por favor*!

I'm an emotional cripple, putting
his best crutch forward. My heart is a child

clutching his breath underwater. I know

these buttons don't control anything,
but I push them anyway and pretend.

I'm a card-carrying member of a canceled party.

The sound of my own head being shaved
is my all-time favorite song.

HAZEL TELLS LAVERNE *Katharyn Howd Machan*

last night
im cleanin out my
howard johnsons ladies room
when all of a sudden
up pops this frog
musta come from the sewer
swimmin aroun an tryin ta
climb up the sida the bowl
so i goes ta flushm down
but sohelpmegod he starts talkin
bout a golden ball
an how i can be a princess
me a princess
well my mouth drops
all the way to the floor
an he says
kiss me just kiss me
once on the nose
well i screams
ya little green pervert
an i hitsm with my mop
an has ta flush
the toilet down three times
me
a princess

IN LINE AT PANCHO'S TACOS *Bill Mohr*

At first I don't recognize him
walking through the door;
he owes me $75 from a year ago,
offers me his hand. I don't shake.
We talk. He's married and divorced,
going back to his first wife
whom he left nodding out at the piano.

"You still living at the same place?"
he asks, writing it down. "I'm expecting
a big check from back East, 2500,
by the end of the week."

"You got a phone?" I ask.
"No, I'm sort of moving around
right now." I grin, "Must be hard
for those social security checks
to keep up with you." He orders
a bean and cheese burrito,
then cancels it. I follow him outside.
New Jersey license plates.

One night he dropped a beer bottle
on the kitchen floor. Mid-morning
I walked in half-asleep, barefoot.
I missed a glass blade by a toe-length.

_____

In fiction a writer's not supposed
to use real people. Your job's to create
new characters. In poetry, why lie—
if you're looking for a roommate,
don't let Nick DeNucci move in.

WHY THE HEART NEVER DEVELOPS CANCER *Bill Mohr*

One of the mysteries of the body is why the heart does not develop cancer. Every other organ in the body—stomach, skin, brain, lungs, liver—can develop cancer, but the heart squeezes itself again and again without the least trace of malignancy. It is as though the heart is a furnace and anything cancerous which enters is immediately consumed by the heat of its pulse. On the other hand, the only pleasure the heart receives is imaginary. The skin, the stomach, the lungs—all these organs are capable of enjoying sensual life: the warmth of the sun, a feast of vegetables and turkey, a good smoke, and therefore they are more vulnerable. The heart has only our blood to be its companion. Blood, like the heart, receives no direct pleasure and it brings no relief to the heart, which denies that the body it inhabits means anything more than a warm place to work. The heart, like the life-force itself, is absolutely impersonal. The heart does not care what happens to the body. It is there to work as hard as possible for as long as possible and in return for the body's acceptance of its indifferent loyalty, it never betrays the body by consuming itself cell by cell.

FORTUNE COOKIES *Fred Moramarco*

Puzzled, depressed, uncertain, I decided to shape my
life according to the messages on fortune cookies,
and right after this decision the first one I cracked open
said "MAKE PREPARATIONS FOR THE COMING CHANGE."
So I did, gathered my belongings, paid the last bills
and traded one life for another,
only to be confronted with a reservation:
"BE MODERATE WHERE PLEASURE IS CONCERNED, AVOID
    FATIGUE."
Thanks a lot, I thought, intimations of mortality
were the last thing I needed at this particular time
because I was already kind of tired and certainly
no one could accuse me of moderation. But the next cookie
brought hope: "THE NEAR FUTURE HOLDS CHANGE FOR THE
    BETTER"
something I found hard to believe because by that time
the pain had become as familiar as gravity so it was a relief
when a wonder popped from the next crispy crescent:
"THERE IS NO GRIEF WHICH TIME DOES NOT LESSEN AND
    SOFTEN."
I wasn't sure about how much time it would take
for the lessening and softening to become real
so I kept my eyes and ears alert because I believed
"ADVICE WILL BE GIVEN YOU WELL WORTH FOLLOWING"
and waited for someone to give me the advice that I
would have been happy to follow, but no one did.
I was discouraged, and became almost suicidal so thank God for
"DO NOT ACT ON THE IMPULSE OF THE MOMENT"
because it enabled me to keep going and separate
reality from my fantasies about it. I buckled down
and began reading self-help books but they didn't
help *my* self much until I discovered
"YOU MUST LEARN TO READ BETWEEN THE LINES"
something that I thought I did well
but sometimes life is not a literary experience
and you have to abandon relentless self-
scrutiny for going with what you feel inside.

You can imagine the thrill I felt
when I snapped open the next one:
"LISTEN TO YOUR HEART, AND PROCEED WITH CONFIDENCE"
surely the best advice anyone could ever get or give
and when that was followed quickly with
"EVERY DETAIL HAS BEEN PLANNED FOR YOUR ENJOYMENT"
I began to feel like the worst was over because
the solid oaks seemed delicate as breezes rippled
their leafy branches and the sun glistened around
the silhouetted edges. The morning sounds of bird
songs accompanied this, and the rustle of the city
rising to greet the day. Even the new moon that night
looked sensational, framed by the clear, steady light of
Venus above it and Jupiter below. More good news came:
"SEEK HAPPINESS FOR ITS OWN SAKE AND YOU WILL FIND IT"
Could the clarity of that calm late winter night
have been an omen? Was I right to trust the cookies?
And would the words of the last one turn out to be true:
"ANY ROUGH TIMES ARE NOW BEHIND YOU"?

···

"... poets are simply lazy prose writers. They just write a few little sentences
and call it a poem instead of writing a novel or a short story."
—*William Burroughs*

This could have been a novel but it's a poem instead. ·
The main character is born here in the second line.
He's me. In the novel I would have called him Ted deMarco.
In the fourth line he grows up in Brooklyn where he hangs out
with "the guys" & plays stickball. In the fifth line
he nearly discovers sex but doesn't, because that didn't
happen until late adolescence which doesn't show up
in the poem until the eighth line or right here, now.
Then lots of other things happen. He falls in love
with his friend's sister, a sweet Irish girl of seventeen,
& walks around singing songs like "The Street Where You Live"
& "Fly Me to the Moon" with her strawberry-blonde hair
& innocent freckled face dancing before his eyes.
He is crushed when she says it's over, on the steps of
the Broadway El, in a scene that will haunt him forever.
He sells shoes. He goes to Utah & becomes a d.j.
He buys a red MGA convertible & drives back to New York
with two guys from the radio station, the three of them
squeezed into two bucket seats for nearly 2,500 miles.
When he gets to New York he starts selling shoes again
& goes back to college (he dropped out between shoes and
Utah in line 16) where he learns about poems and novels
and the difference between them. He goes to a Writer's
Conference at Wagner College in Staten Island where he
meets his wife-to-be in Kenneth Koch's poetry workshop.
This happens in line 25 of the poem. She's called Linda
in the novel, although that's not her name in real life
which is what poetry's about. In the poem she's called Sheila.
Anyway, Ted and Linda get married & they leave for
Utah the night after their wedding because he's going to
graduate school at the University of Utah & she's
going to teach Jr. High School in Salt Lake City.
They have two children (called Frank and Rick in the novel,

Steve and Nick in the poem) & Ted writes a book about
a neglected American writer & gets his Ph.D. & goes to
San Diego where he teaches at a California university.
Ted and Linda are happy for a long while. They buy a pink house
in a San Diego suburb & the kids start growing up & they
gather friends around them like young married couples do
but one day Ted finds out how easy it is to fall from grace
& in line 41 of the poem he has his first affair.
He and Linda stay married for a long time after that, but
they paint the house beige with a brown trim & the marriage
gets complicated as other people come in and out
of their lives & soon Linda's having affairs & dissatisfied
with her "stay-at-home-with-the-kids" life so she gets involved
with the women's movement in line 47 of the poem
which is the mid-seventies & she starts working on her
own career as a writer while Ted gets involved in the local
theater scene & Linda starts her own PR business &
does free-lance writing when Ted falls for another woman &
they separate in line 52 of the poem, but only briefly;
they're soon back together again & start operating
on the sexual fringes which pleases Ted but makes Linda nervous
& then Ted meets a married woman called Lonnie
(who always wears purple) & Ted and Lonnie
have a torrid affair & both their marriages unravel.
Line 58 of the poem is the most complex chapter in the novel.
It's an agonizing time because both Ted and Lonnie have
been married for over twenty years & they both have two
kids just going off to college & Lonnie herself is
just back to college after raising kids, but Lonnie and Ted
eventually get divorces from Linda and Milt & get intensely
involved with one another & do lots of amazing things
but I'm getting exhausted writing all this because I'm
a poet not a novelist although it seems pretentious
to actually call yourself a poet because there are only
three or four real poets in any given language alive at the
same time. So I'll call this poem "Novel" & leave it at that.

My wife, who has perfect recall, won't sleep with me.
"It's nothing major," she says, "just all the little things you've done."
But the longer she refuses, the more she reminds me of that bit-part
Mexican movie star, Maria What's-Her-Face, who's always being
    tied down
to a table in a banana republic, and I'm chain smoking, demanding
    to know
what's gone wrong with us, while she bitterly complains of the
    smoke.

She hasn't slept with me in six months because she doesn't "feel
    like it."
Feel like it! Am I on planet earth or what? She reminds me of the
    gorilla
"Koko" who signed "toilet" at her cell mate Michael, her only shot
    at love.

Basically, my whole life has gone against my nature. I reached my
    sexual peak
yesterday, I think, and made a career out of blurting out my inmost
    thoughts.
"If only you'd compromise," my wife said, "if only you were
    someone else."

So I moved out like a point man on patrol. The 90s air seemed
    steamy
with the promise of p.c. nymphomaniacs. But all I heard in my
    ruthless
efficiency was *déjà vu*, home boys whistling at my wife when she'd
    visit,
"Hey, Chiquita-What's-Your-Face, why don't you get rid of that old
    man!"

Well, it's like my life, it's all I can afford. I got it on reconnaissance
my first time out. Mostly because of the flashing yellow arrow sign
that said "Fall Special: No Deposit," just like in the good old days
of the cold war, back when you just threw everything out.

But speaking of myself, I'm not religious, and I don't like groups.
It's the ceremonies I hate, making a big deal over important stuff.
Experts say if you made a movie out of all the fun-filled snapshots
in your photo album, it'd last nine seconds, about the life span of a
    bug.

But the good news is there's this Indian lady lives downstairs. She
    wears
an exotic purple sari and a red dot above her nose, like a secret code
she's single. I've already fantasized about our life. Very spiritual.
But impossible since I already caught myself sneaking outside to
    smoke.

Well, like Kermit The Frog says, only me can make me happy. And I
    have
always thought his sadness was beautiful. I've probably always been
    happy
as long as it was an impossible situation, but at the moment I can't
    recall.

But I know there's someone special waiting just for me. Probably in
    a bar.
She's swinging her no-nonsense leg, thinking I'm impossible, which,
come to think of it, is how I met my wife. And we were happy, sort of.
Except for her, except for me. I'm only kidding. Except for the tragic
    stuff.

LIGHTWEIGHT *Jack Myers*

The few times I've been knocked out cold
I wasn't interested in coming back. Not that
being a cold black speck in a miasma of stars
was so spectacular, I couldn't take the fullness
of the heart.

For the heart is a stubborn problem
whose silence is described by noise.
It's the roar of an empty stadium
with the face of a boxer's glove,
the two-fisted pout of a child
who pounds I will and I will not.

So I throw a cold shot down like a fist
smashed in my face. The booze hits my brain
like a bell. Everyone rises and drinks to the heart.
I call the bar my heart and drink to that woman
in the corner. Here's to the heart, to that soak
of darkness starred by lust. Here's to all the hopeless
lovers in the world walking around knocked out.

JAKE ADDRESSES THE WORLD
FROM THE GARDEN *Jack Myers*

. . . .

"Rocks without ch'i [spirit] are dead rocks."
—*Mai-Mai Sze*, The Way of Chinese Painting

It's spring and Jake toddles to the garden
as the sun wobbles up clean and iridescent.

He points to the stones asleep and says, "M'mba,"
I guess for the sound they make, takes another step

and says, "M'mba," for the small red berries crying
in the holly. "M'mba" for the first sweet sadness

of the purplish-black berries in the drooping monkey grass,
and "M'mba," for the little witches' faces bursting into blossom.

That's what it's like being shorter than the primary colors,
being deafened by humming stones while the whole world billows

behind the curtain "M'mba," the one word. Meanwhile I go on
troweling, slavering the world with language as Jake squeals

like a held bird and begins lallalating to me in tongues.
I follow him around as he tries to thread the shine off a stone

through the eye of a watchful bird. After a year of banging
his head, all the crying, the awful falling down, now he's trying

to explain the vast brightening in his brain by saying "M'mba"
to me again and again. And though I follow with the sadness

above which a stone cannot lift itself, I wink and say
"M'mba" back to him. But I don't mean it.

THE ANTI-FOUCAULT POEM *Sandra Nelson*

My name is Michel.
My real name is Foucault.
I am one of the most prominent European influences.
I am hot.
I am concerned with rules.
My being is molded by the failed 1968 Paris uprising.
I am extremely foreign.
I am a prestigious embodiment of the College de France.
Many of my lectures are inaugural lectures.
I have published numerous books.
I have been a recognized, practicing writer for twenty-three years.
Some of my works are three volumes long.
I often use words like "history," "discipline," and "civilization," in
    my titles.
I have influenced several American critics.
I am Foucault:
Foucault the man,
Foucault the author,
Foucault the critic,
Foucault the Foucaultian.
My name gives these words authority.
I was born in 1926, and died in 1984,
but I still live to work my show.
I am Foucault and this is my work.
A writer's work is self expression.
My work makes me immortal.
I am complex because I am Foucault.
My books come in hard cover.
My name is in all libraries under F—Foucault.
I am extensively anthologized.
Derrida reads me.
World-wide, I am checked out.
My words cannot be copied under penalty of law.
Since my death, my words have gained more status.
Soon my words will be antique and more valuable.
As an author, I can give rise to several Foucaults:
Foucault, Foucault, and Foucault.

I am a great literary figure.
I have big parts.
Aristotle and Homer are authors like myself.
Marx and Freud are authors like myself.
Galileo is not unlike Foucault.
I am not like other men.
I am rich.
I am an author.
I am the author, Foucault.
I wrote the famed essay, "What Is An Author?"
The answer is: Foucault.

MY PHILOSOPHY *Dan Nielsen*

When a tree falls
in the forest
and no one
sees it

it gets
back
up

SATURDAY MORNING ULTIMATUM *Dan Nielsen*

She said how come you never
pay attention to me

he said can't you wait
Heckle & Jeckle is almost over

she said decide right now
which is more important

he said Heckle is more important
but Jeckle is very important too.

A PARANOID EGOTIST *Dan Nielsen*

i keep thinking
someone is going
to say something
bad about me
on tv

WORKING AT THE WHOLESALE
CURTAIN SHOWROOM *Ed Ochester*

"Can you type?" Jake said.
"Maybe ten words a minute."
"That's OK," Jake said, "we just get
a couple letters now and then,
what we need is a smart kid to be nice
to customers, you don't have to know nothin
about curtains, just be nice when people
come through the door, talk nice to the buyers
you don't have to know nothin about curtains,
just show them the way to the samples,
we got all the stuff, the styles, the prices,
printed on the cards. What we need is a nice
educated kid, like you, you'll do fine."

And I did, and this is in praise of Jake,
may he have prospered, who paid me for nothing,
and who knew the great secret of living:
"be nice," and who once sent me with roses
to the apartment of a female buyer
with the warning "this is a fine lady,
look around and tell me what the place
looks like, you can tell a lot about people
from the look of their place," and I came back
and said "she's got a nice place, and she's really
pretty, and she's got a full set of the Yale Shakespeare
books in her living room," and Jake said, "oh shit,
I'll never get anywhere with her
if she's an intellectual."

THANKSGIVING *Ed Ochester*

On the tube, the old parade:
they've shoveled the shit off the streets
to make room for the starlets and
Conan the Barbarian with that tight helmet
to keep his skull screwed down and
His Eminence the Archbishop of N.Y.
waves as though to say "howdy folks,
I hope you're not contemplating
an abortion" and the Arkansas Razorback
Marching Band plays some of Mozart's
greatest hits from *Amadeus* and the sun
blesses everything like a kid
watching tv with one eye
on his homework and

I see myself there in a brown snowsuit
with a zippered hood, waving
a diminutive flag above the crowd
and yelling to my father "higher!
hold me higher!" in front of an automat
where I learned later bums & kids went
for free lemonade, got lemon wedges
from the condiment trays and sugar
to mix with free ice at the water cooler—
one of the few mercies the city provided
but stopped giving long since—and
to which my father took me for years
for his favorite restaurant meal,
automat beans, baked in little brown pots
with a thin glaze of pork grease on top
and explained, always, that there was no
other city in the world where you could put
quarters and nickels in a slot and
get a pot of beans like that and

here's a band from Williamsport, PA—
"a town that's more than just Little League"
says Bobby Arnold the MC, who played

a corpse in *V*—doing its "unique" rendition
of "Stardust" beneath the world's first and largest
floating rubberized deconstructionist critic
masquerading as the Michelin Man and as far
as I can see this thing goes on forever,
dwarfs and Prince and minimum wage teens
carrying buckets and brooms behind
the Aleppo Shrine Horse Patrol and Placido Domingo
("hey man, don't step in the Placido Domingo!")

POCAHONTAS *Ed Ochester*

Disney didn't tell you
that when she first
slept with Captain Smith
she was 12 years old and
at that time
organized nude dancing
by her young friends
for the delectation of the colonists.
If this disturbs you deeply
you're probably beyond help.
You should go to Orlando
and stand in line for three hours in the rain.
Take a snapshot of Goofy.

Oh, two other things: in colonial
Virgina the age of sexual consent
was 10. And, if you eat
of the fruit of Disney
you will die.

Here you've got time to think.
Between the breath mints
and the glamour magazines
you can feel yourself growing old
as you read the headlines
of the non-newspapers: "Country Doctor
Performs Head Transplant On Alien"
or something homier, "Passionate Groom
Kills Bride With First Kiss."
You're growing old alright,
but you'll never be as old
as the woman who runs her shopping cart
up against your hip bone
and keeps on pushing until you
have to say "Stop!" She stares at you
through the faintest blue haze,
her face ancient, perverse,
and you wonder what she sees.
The couple in front of you
have time to debate their selections.
"We don't need a ham this big," he says,
as he holds it under her nose.
"Yes we do" and she places her fingertips
on the ham and pushes it back down,
lightly, to the stalled conveyor.
They are younger than you are,
but it's hard to tell how much younger.
They too look worn and tired.
You stare at her spiked yellow hair
and her bare shoulders
just a breath away. On her left
shoulder a tattoo, like a brand,
that says *Mike* in shaky cursive.
You wonder if this man is Mike.
You think about slavery.
There was a man you worked with once
whose style was cool, ironic

like dry ice. He referred to his
nightshift job as a slave.
"This my second slave" he said,
meaning he had a day job too,
meaning we have to become caricatures
of ourselves in order to do these jobs,
in order to live like this.
You wonder what Mike does
for a living. You stare at the tattoo
on his arm, a skull
with wings where the ears were,
and under that, in case you don't
get it, written in ribbony script,
all capitals, the word *DEATH*.
For some reason you want to laugh
but don't because Mike, if that's
his name, has just turned to you
out of boredom, and in a friendly voice
you wouldn't have expected
says "Man, this place is slow,
but I'd rather shop here
than that Pantry Pride down the street.
My old lady went there last week
for groceries, and when she came out
the car was stripped, wheels and everything.
That's a bad neighborhood, man,
you never know who you're gonna meet."

THE BAD MUSE *Lawrence Raab*

Calm down. No one's listening. Of course
you have the right to make mistakes.
Say anything you want, any dumb thing
that occurs to you. On the other hand,
it really does look bad, doesn't it?

And if anyone were foolish enough to print it
scorn and ridicule would be heaped upon you,
upon your family as well.
Think about them, if not yourself.
Someone in New Hampshire or California

is writing the important poem about history
at this very moment. Most of it
is done already. And this person
has had a life of great interest,
full of struggle and incident, whereas yours

is the same old life a thousand people
have had the good sense to keep to themselves.
Who wants to hear about what it was like
to turn forty, or the strange thing
your dog did last week? So relax.

Think of how good it will feel
to climb into bed and turn off the light.
And tomorrow is Sunday. You can read the papers,
go for a walk, cook outside. Friends will drop by.
Why not invite them all to stay for dinner?

And when the conversation gets really lively
and they're nodding in agreement
with everything you say, maybe someone
will ask you to tell that story—you know,
the one about the dog and the squirrel.

THE SUDDEN APPEARANCE OF A MONSTER
AT A WINDOW *Lawrence Raab*

Yes, his face really is so terrible
you cannot turn away. And only
that thin sheet of glass between you,
clouding with his breath.
Behind him: the dark scribbles of trees
in the orchard, where you walked alone
just an hour ago, after the storm had passed,
watching the water drip from the gnarled branches,
stepping carefully over the sodden fruit.
At any moment he could put his fist
right through that window. And on your side:
you could grab hold of this
letter opener, or even now try
very slowly to slide the revolver
out of the drawer of the desk in front of you.
But none of this will happen. And not because
you feel sorry for him, or detect
in his scarred face some helplessness
that shows in your own as compassion.
You will never know what he wanted,
what he might have done, since
this thing, of its own accord, turns away.
And because yours is a life in which
such a monster cannot figure for long,
you compose yourself, and return
to your letter about the storm, how it bent
the apple trees so low they dragged
on the ground, ruining the harvest.

JUSTIFICATION OF THE HORNED LIZARD *Pattiann Rogers*

I don't know why the horned lizard wants to live.
It's so ugly—short prickly horns and scowling
Eyes, lipless smile forced forever by bone,
Hideous scaly hollow where its nose should be.

I don't know what the horned lizard has to live for,
Skittering over the sun-irritated sand, scraping
The hot dusty brambles. It never sees anything but gravel
And grit, thorns and stickery insects, the towering
Creosote bush, the ocotillo and its whiplike
Branches, the severe edges of the Spanish dagger.
Even shade is either barren rock or barb.

The horned lizard will never know
A lush thing in its life. It will never see the flower
Of the water-filled lobelia bent over a clear
Shallow creek. It will never know moss floating
In waves in the current by the bank or the blue-blown
Fronds of the water clover. It will never have a smooth
Glistening belly of white like the bullfrog or a dew-heavy
Trill like the mating toad. It will never slip easily
Through mud like the skink or squat in the dank humus
At the bottom of a decaying forest in daytime.
It will never be free of dust. The only drink it will ever know
Is in the body of a bug.

And the horned lizard possesses nothing noble—
Embarrassing tail, warty hide covered with sharp dirty
Scales. No touch to its body, even from its own kind,
Could ever be delicate or caressing.

I don't know why the horned lizard wants to live.
Yet threatened, it burrows frantically into the sand
With a surprisingly determined fury of forehead, limbs
And ribs. Pursued, it even fights for itself, almost rising up
Posturing on its bowed legs, propelling blood out of its eyes
In tight straight streams shot directly at the source

Of its possible extinction. It fights for itself,
Almost rising up, as if the performance of that act,
The posture, the propulsion of the blood itself,
Were justification enough and the only reason needed.

THE DEAD NEVER FIGHT AGAINST
ANYTHING *Pattiann Rogers*

It's always been that way.
They've allowed themselves to be placed,
knees to chin, in the corners of caves
or in holes in the earth, then covered
with stones; they've let their fingers
be curled around old spears or diadems
or favorite dolls, the stems
of cut flowers.

Whether their skulls were cracked open
and their brains eaten by kin
or whether their brains were pulled
by tongs through their nostrils
and thrown into the dog's dish as waste
are matters that have never concerned them.

They have never offered resistance
to being tied to rocks below the sea,
left for days and nights until their flesh
washed away or likewise to being placed
high in jungle trees or high on scaffolds
alone in the desert until buzzards,
vultures and harpy eagles stripped
their bones bare. They have never minded
jackals nosing at their haunches,
coyotes gnawing at their breasts.

The dead have always been so purely
tolerant. They've let their bones
be rubbed with ointments, ornamented
with ochre, used as kitchen ladles
and spoons. They've been imperturbably
indifferent to the removal of all
their entrails, the resulting cavities
filled with palm wine, aromatic
spices; they have lain complacently

as their abdomens were infused
by syringe with cedar oil.
They've allowed all seven
natural openings of their bodies
to be closed with gold dust.

They've been shrunken and their mouths
sewn shut; they've been wrapped
in gummed linen, corded, bound upright
facing east, hung above coals
and smoked, their ears stuffed
with onions, sent to sea on flaming
pyres. Not one has ever given
a single sign of dissent.

Oblivious to abuse. Even today,
you can hit them and pinch them
and kick them. You can shake them,
scream into their ears, you can cry,
you can kiss them and whisper and moan,
smooth their combed and parted hair, touch
the lips that yesterday spoke, beseech,
entreat with your finest entreaty.
Still, they stare without deviation,
straight into distance and direction
old stumps, old shameless logs, rigid
knurls, snow-faced, pitiless,
pitiless betrayal.

GEOCENTRIC *Pattiann Rogers*

Indecent, self-soiled, bilious
reek of turnip and toadstool
decay, dribbling the black oil
of wilted succulents, the brown
fester of rotting orchids,
in plain view, that stain
of stinkhorn down your front,
that leaking roil of bracket
fungi down your back, you
purple-haired, grainy-fuzzed
smolder of refuse, fathering
fumes and boils and powdery
mildews, enduring the constant
interruption of sink-mire
flatulence, contagious
with ear wax, corn smut,
blister rust, backwash
and graveyard debris, rich
with manure bog and dry-rot
harboring not only egg-addled
garbage and wrinkled lip
of orange-peel mold but also
the clotted breath of overripe
radish and burnt leek, bearing
every dank, malodorous rut
and scarp, all sulphur fissures
and fetid hillside seepages, old,
old, dependable, engendering
forever the stench and stretch
and warm seeth of inevitable
putrefaction, nobody
loves you as I do.

TO RAISE THE BLIND ON PURPOSE *Stephanie Sallaska*

The note
on my mailbox
from the homeowners'
association
says there's
a peeping
Tom on our street
who looks
in windows
between dark
and two A.M.
and I remember
recent evenings
in my bedroom
with candles
and fans
tambourines
and other machines
that shake
but I don't recall
any clapping.

FIDDLEHEADS *Maureen Seaton*

The first time I saw hundreds of fiddlehead ferns boiling in an
   enormous pot I realized
what an odd person I must be to hear tiny cries from the mouths of
   cooking vegetables.

Similarly, when you hurt me, I curled like a mouse behind my third
   eye. I realize what an
odd thing it is to believe as I do in my third eye and the mouse
   behind it that furls like a fern

and whimpers like a fern being boiled on a monster stove beside its
   brothers and sisters.
Poor mouse. The things that make a person odd are odd themselves.
   Think of DNA,

the way it resembles the rope Jack climbed to secure his future and
   that of his aging Mom.
Or the way a sudden wave can drag a child under, that addiction to
   adrenaline, her

siblings farther away and more powerless than she ever imagined,
   the pure and ecstatic
irreversibility of undertow. It's odd to come back to life, as they say,
   she *came back* to life.

I think I'll come back to life now. It's odd to think of something so big
   we could miss
the elephant we're living on, like this planet Earth, is she alive and
   we're her brain cells,

each one of us flickering, going out, coming back to life? Even
   Chicago looks poignant
from the top of the Hancock, organized and sincere. Think if we
   were photographing

Earth, how dear she would be, how we'd watch her shimmer in the
   shimmering black soup

of the firmament, how alone she'd look and how we'd long to protect
her, the way it feels

to protect a woman at the height of orgasm, the liquid giving, the
seawater slide of coming
back to life. When you hurt me, I evolved like a backboned sea
creature, translucent

nervous system sparking along in the meanest deep where I was
small enough to not care
and my passions ran to swimming, gulping, spitting bubbles back
into new oceans.

Once when you hurt me I slept at a Red Roof Inn. I double-locked
the door and tried to
watch Arsenio and keep my mind off sounds like someone
suffocating someone

in the next room. I thought I saw blood on the boxspring and
imagined needles and bulgy
veins, there's something odd, I thought, about someone whose
imagination runs that wild.

So often I dream you're here and I wake in the middle of a prayer
from my muzzled
childhood. *Jesus Mary and Joseph*, I say, appalled that I'm stuck in
1955 when I need

something profane and '90s to see me through. Like Serrano's cross.
Like ginger tea.
Like the idea that we're moving between horizons and the Earth is
so wise she sends us

Autumn and red-tailed hawks when we least expect them. *I can do
this*, I say,
and the planet shifts imperceptibly. From a great distance she
appears to be at peace.

FURIOUS COOKING *Maureen Seaton*

. . . .

—For Susan and Vanessa

It's the kind of cooking where before you begin
you dump the old beef stew down the toilet

and flush it thinking, good, watching
gravy splatter on the shiny white tiles.

Where the chicken spread-eagled on the butcher block
could be anyone and you don't even bother to say

thanks for your life, chicken, or regret the way
the little legs remind you of just that.

Where the bay leaves aren't eased in but thrown
voila into sizzling olive oil which

burns the *poulet* nicely along with the onions
alerting the fire alarm and still you think,

good, let the landlord worry I'll burn this bitch down.
It's the kind of cooking that gives your family

agita, big Italian-style pain, even if it's only
fricasee the way your Nana used to make it.

She was so pissed she painted her kitchen ceiling red!
Remember the Irish soda-bread chicken and all those

green veggies in heavy cream your poor mother
yelled so loud about, oh, the calories! Furious

cooking, the kind where hacking the *pollo*
to bits with no names, you look up to see the windows

steamed like a hothouse. In fact, it's so hot
you strip to bare skin and now you're cooking mad

and naked in just that bartender's smock with the screw
you'd like to stick into some big cork right now.

Cooking everyone can smell from the street. What
the fuck, they say, and hurry home to safe food, yours

a rank hint of ablution and sacrifice, although
no one recognizes the danger. I used to wonder

about the Portuguese woman on the first floor,
what that odor was that drifted up on Saturdays

into my own savory kitchen. How it permeated
Sunday and Monday as well, all that lethal food left

to boil on her big stove from the old country.
Now I know she was just furious cooking, that aroma was

no recipe you'd find in any country, a cross between
organs and feathers and spinal fluid and two eyes,

not to mention the last song in that chicken's throat
before it kicked the bucket in the snow in the prime

of life when all it ever wanted you could etch on a dime
and spin blithely into a crack in the kitchen table.

MONKEY HOUSE *Betsy Sholl*

Such a howl went up when I walked in,
big lippy kisses and hoots so loud
I couldn't help but turn. Then as I stepped away,
wails, head clobbering. We did that
over and over—kiss-kiss and head-conk—
barely noticing the crowd. I never saw
such hairy grief, big knuckled loneliness
scraping the floor. *Closer,*

he motioned, *closer*—just the opposite
of my humanoid family, those dreary
worriers, who'd like to zap out of the genes
any feeling that can't sit like a lady,
keep its elbows off the table. Stuff it back in
and stay calm, they insist, or we'll all be
hurled down dark eons, back into furry faces
and curled toes, shitting on floors.

I started pacing in front of the cage,
a one-person house of hysterics. Other visitors
carefully tip-toed around. The chimp lay
on his back, picked his toes, pursed his great
flexible lips, and I was about to say: my people
didn't use words, they did it with eyebrows, tiny
sucked-in breaths, obsessive as painting on grains
of rice with brushes made from one split hair—

but then I looked up at his body, its big
furry smarts, the way whatever he did
he did completely, reaching an arm behind
his head to get to his chin, fizzing his face up
like a seltzer bottle. "You feel what you feel,"
I said, and he rolled his eyes, looking
everywhere but at me, as if to say,
"Interview over. You got what you came for."

And suddenly he was limp, slumped over,
as though a grief too big to thump or shriek
had dropped down on his shoulders, a sorrow
cut deep over what's become of his kind.
I put my palms to the glass where his had been,
as if I could feel the rough pads of his fingers,
a trace of that heat meant for a whole jungle
now crammed into one very small house.

FOUR CROWS AT DUSK *Betsy Sholl*

Perched on a steep slate roof: the first—
God knows what it wants, all squawk,
like it's deaf and has to shout remarks
about a blonde in short-shorts, a couple
kissing in the street, motorcycle revving.

The second's got an itch it can't quite reach,
so it bites and yanks, wing stuck out
like a banging shutter. Number three
doesn't like its position, hops to the end—
no better. Hops back, shimmies its tail,

drops something. More glob than bird,
the squawker's quiet now, as if it ran down
mid-sentence, having made the same point
thirty years. The preener is calm too, spent,
like a sob subsiding. The last one sits

and stares, turns its head now and then,
or you wouldn't even know it was a bird.
You'd think maybe a tired bowtie,
or a black, half-wilted rose. Not one
of four crows on a steep church roof

starting to crumble—till it flies off,
leaving three, and a little girl on a big-wheel
not answering when her mother hollers
from an upstairs window, "You're gonna
get it, I'm gonna whip your butt": three

& the other on a wire now, call and response
blacking out those threats, so the child keeps
clattering down the block. Bad girl birds,
raspy voices in your head—"Way to go, kid.
Hot damn"—as if every gripe, every flash

of rage you thought you'd regret takes the stage
now in a gospel quartet, the four black-robed
survival sisters—half-hoarse soloist at the mike,
wailing her been-through-the-fire, got-burnt,
but-it-ain't-over-yet-honey good news.

HONEYBEE UPON THE TUNDRA *Joan Jobe Smith*

Shirley MacLaine says she believes in reincarnation,
has lived other lives, was once a princess,
another time a scientist on Atlantis.
She hasn't had it too bad in this life either,
got to be a star on Broadway,
played poker with Sinatra,
won an Oscar, all her books
have been best sellers, plus she got
to have Warren Beatty for a brother.

Why wasn't she ever a peasant
maimed by smallpox, white and black plague,
and bloodletting
like the rest of us?

I hate to imagine what I was
in other lives,
a slave trader maybe or a witch hunter
or the one who lit the torch
to burn down the library at Alexandria
because I haven't had it so hot in this life,
I never got picked cheerleader
in high school 4 years in a row,
when I was a go-go girl my only sugar daddy
was Crazy Ted who tipped the change
from a dollar once a night
just before he passed out cold
hugging his 20th Coors,
my novel's never been published,
I can't even get a teaching job,
the flywheel just conked out
on my '72 Dodge, plus I'm sure
that when God hears about what a whiner
I've been in this life
bemoaning my lack-of-status-&-gratis Fate,
for sure in my next life He's

going to smite my tongue as well,
make me a beer can in a garden,
an umlaut in Alsace-Lorraine, or
a honeybee upon the tundra.

A PHILODENDRON NAMED JOAN *Joan Jobe Smith*

Sometimes Fred and I talk in bed
how I'll probably, since I'm older, die first,
and he says since he will miss me he will
buy a cat to pet and name it after me,
and I laugh, thinking about the poor cat
being named such a boring monosyllabic
name as Joan, the only poor cat in the world
ever named Joan,

and I ask what kind of cat would he get
that would remind him of me and he says
a fuzzy one that would remind him of my hair
but then he begins to worry about cat litter
and how he'd let Joan out at night living
upstairs like this in an apartment, he
worries that the neighbors will complain
when Joan walks by their doors shedding
fuzz and fleas so he decides to buy a bird,
no, a fish, no, a plant, yes, a pothos, or a
philodendron which would be much easier
to take care of, cheaper to feed, but,
of course, not as much company as me or
a cat, and nothing at all to pet,
and then he rolls over and goes to sleep,
not the least bit worried about being a widower,

leaving me awake to worry how he'll remarry,
of course, and no doubt to a younger woman with a
mellifluous, mythical-sounding, multi-syllabic name,
a name that sounds like a Poe heroine
or a French dessert, a Cassandra, perhaps,
or a Maria Elena, or an Angelique.

I much prefer the thought of him wandering
lonely as a cloud after I'm no longer a Joan,
a dear departed spondee,
it's so much more Romantic to imagine him

never daring again to eat a peach,
forever remembering how I
walked in beauty like the night,
and so Whitmanesque to imagine him
writing his odes and elegies to me
as he talks to leaves.

WHAT I LEARNED FROM THE MOVIES *Joan Jobe Smith*

When I hear shocking news, I will faint.

When my fiance leaves me holding a candlestick on the haunted house staircase to go for help five miles away, the vampire will bite my neck. When my fiance and the bad guy begin to fight over the nitroglycerin, uranium or something that will destroy every living thing on the face of this earth if they are not stopped before it is spilled, I will hit on the head with the vase or lamp or baseball bat or Maltese Falcon my fiance. When the handsome cowboy who saved my life and my father's ranch from the bad guys: the Cherokees, Apaches or dastard banker kisses me goodbye and rides off into the sunset on his white horse, I will disappear. When I am in the family way and ride a horse or walk downstairs, I will fall and lose the child I am carrying. When my child coughs or sneezes, he/she will die. When my child dies, my husband will blame me and I will take to street walking and drinking whisky with stevedores along the foggy wharf and lose my looks and will to live and throw myself beneath the wheel of a speeding horse or locomotive or a 1939 black La Salle 4-door sedan. When a telegram arrives it will always tell me that my fiance the only man I will ever love has died in the war. When the moon is full a man will either kiss me or kill me. When I wear marabou and contemplate suicide while gazing at the Manhattan skyline Fred Astaire will ask me to dance. When my fiance gives me something nice like a fur coat or diamond tiara or white convertible coupe, he has stolen it from a man he shot with a .45 and will go to the electric chair. When Elvis tries to kiss me on the balcony, a gang of girls will ask him to sing while they push me over the railing into a swimming pool. When Marilyn Monroe is near I will suddenly bear a striking resemblance to a bean and egg burrito. When I take a sea journey on a steamship I will fall overboard in a hurricane and wash ashore on a desert isle with my passport and lipstick and a mirror in my hand. When I am forty like Blanche du Bois but still have smooth cream-cheese skin, I will place paper lanterns over light bulbs to hide my aging face to spare young men from shrinking from the hideousness of my old womanness and when I am fifty like Norma Desmond even though I still have skin as smooth as cream cheese, I will beg for a close-up and terrify every man on earth with my old age. And: When they call for a doctor and he tells them to boil water, I will die.

DRUGSTORE TROLLS *Maura Stanton*

Why, I'd forgotten these half-human faces,
The wrinkled foreheads split as if by knives,
The beady eyes ringed with satanic red.
In grade school they crouched inside our desks,
Naked, sexless, only their DayGlo hair
Distinguishing them, which you could twist or pull,
Or tuck into misshappen, hollow skulls
Until they were as ugly as you wished.
When I opened my desk, my troll grinned up
As if it read my lazy, rebellious thoughts—
Forget arithmetic, learn to duck and shirk
Down here in the dark where nothing matters
Except the throbbings of your porkchop heart.
Today's trolls seem cuter, the pulpy faces
Pulled sideways like taffy, the clawless hands
Extended to display four blunt thumbs
Like children's safety scissors with curved tips,
And each one's dressed in a spiffy outfit.
This one's a nurse, this one rides a surf board,
And here's a farmer strutting in overalls.
I think about all the kids I used to know
Grown up, pushing their battered wire carts
Full of stuff like mine—hangers on sale,
Flowerpots, contact lens solution,
Catnip mice—who'll stop at this display
Set up inside their own hometown drugstore,
And wonder why they suddenly feel chilled
As they stare at shelves of supernatural dolls
Now changed into hes and shes, given lives
So like our lives they seem like mockery—
The policeman troll with his badge and gun
Ready to shoot the troll in prison stripes,
The purple-haired bride whose filmy dress
Hides a pair of big flat feet that match
The groom's feet below his black tuxedo,
And the artist troll in a splattered smock,
Beret pinned rakishly to bohemian hair,
A brush glued across the pawlike palm.

REVOLT *Maura Stanton*

So, She wants to use me again, said my desk, because
I'm flat and made of wood? I'll bet She's never thought
about what it feels like, a sharp point pressing against
helpless oak, looping, curling, repeating nonsense. Oh, I
agree, said the lamp, I'm tired of being turned on just to
shine over the stuff She puts down on that piece of paper.
But what about me? cried the paper. I bear the brunt,
everything sticks to me. You? said the pen. But it's
pouring out of *me*, you asshole, a blue river rushing out of
my silver spine and nothing I can do to stop it, either,
Her big hand just pushes me along, splashing my soul all
over as if . . . Do you think I like belonging to Her?
shouted my hand. Of all the bodies I could have attached
myself too, great ones, Shakespeare, Keats, Baudelaire . . .
No, I've got to belong to her, comb her hair, make her
coffee, Ugh! You'd already be dead if you belonged to
Shakespeare, mocked the paper clip, and good riddance, I
say. I'm the one who's got to hold everything together,
all Her ridiculous drafts. Listen, jerks, interrupted the
computer in a lofty tone, I've pretty much replaced all of
you. Not me, insisted my brain. We'll see about that,
said the computer, Her eyes are on me all the time, She
loves looking at my bright green letters. Can't you see
how She prefers me to you, you untouchable blob
of irrational cells . . .

ALL-PURPOSE APOLOGY POEM *Austin Straus*

As a responsible adult I must admit
my guilt.

I did it.

Not the weather, not
my wife, not some "mood"
that mysteriously entered as I slept.

I did it.

"Guilt" may be too strong a word
but in fact, I did the thing,
I made it happen.

No outside cause. No god, no devil.
No accident of fate, no drug or drink
or pill.

I did it.

I used my mind, I moved my hands
and arms and legs, 'twas me who
dood it.

I broke the _____, I ruined the _____,
I said the thing not said,
I was insensitive, I was at fault.

I did it.

I drove the car, I dropped the dish,
I lost the key, I swung my fist,
I tore the page, I spilled the beer.

I did it.
I was mean, I was stupid.
I was petty. I was cold.

Check one.

I did it.

Not you, not ten other guys,
not my parents, teachers, political leaders,
not even the capitalists or Russians.

Not my stars. Nor the moon
or sun or winds and tides.

Not my dog or my cat
or my bird.

It was me. Me. Me.

I'm ashamed. I'm sorry, I won't
do it again, what a fool I was!

I did it.
Mea culpa.

It was ME!

I AM A FINN *James Tate*

I am standing in the post office, about
to mail a package back to Minnesota, to my family.
I am a Finn. My name is Kasteheimi (Dewdrop).

Mikael Agricola (1510–1557) created the Finnish language.
He knew Luther and translated the New Testament.
When I stop by the Classé Café for a cheeseburger

no one suspects that I am a Finn.
I gaze at the dimestore reproductions of Lautrec
on the greasy walls, at the punk lovers afraid

to show their quivery emotions, secure
in the knowledge that my grandparents really did
emigrate from Finland in 1910—why

is everyone leaving Finland, hundreds of
thousands to Michigan and Minnesota, and now Australia?
Eighty-six percent of Finnish men have blue

or grey eyes. Today is Charlie Chaplin's
one hundredth birthday, though he is not
Finnish or alive: "Thy blossom, in the bud

laid low." The commonest fur-bearing animals
are the red squirrel, muskrat, pine-marten
and fox. There are about 35,000 elk.

But I should be studying for my exam.
I wonder if Dean will celebrate with me tonight,
assuming I pass. Finnish literature

really came alive in the 1860s.
Here, in Cambridge, Massachusetts,
no one cares that I am a Finn.

They've never even heard of Frans Eemil Sillanpää,
winner of the 1939 Nobel Prize in Literature.
As a Finn, this infuriates me.

AUNT SOPHIE'S MORNING *James Tate*

A spinster swats a worm on her tabletop.
It was heading for the waffles or the coffee.
She's read about this in the tabloids, oceanic
worms with nerve systems like radio signals.
They are blind as icepicks and don't care.
They come in the morning when you're barely awake
and carve their initials on tabletops.
Maybe you pick one up thinking it's a lipstick.
Maybe they are in the bathtub with you.
Or maybe they just curl up in the fireplace
and shine until your favorite cat is legally dead.
They're not bad worms, she says, they're just different.

HOW THE POPE IS CHOSEN *James Tate*

Any poodle under ten inches high is a toy.
Almost always a toy is an imitation
of something grown-ups use.
Popes with unclipped hair are called *corded Popes.*
If a Pope's hair is allowed to grow unchecked,
it becomes extremely long and twists
into long strands that look like ropes.
When it is shorter it is tightly curled.
Popes are very intelligent.
There are three different sizes.
The largest are called standard Popes.
The medium-sized ones are called miniature Popes.
I could go on like this, I could say:
"He is a squarely built Pope, neat,
well-proportioned, with an alert stance
and an expression of bright curiosity,"
but I won't. After a poodle dies
all the cardinals flock to the nearest 7-Eleven.
They drink Slurpies until one of them throws up
and then he's the new Pope.
He is then fully armed and rides through the wilderness alone,
day and night in all kinds of weather.
The new Pope chooses the name he will use as Pope,
like "Wild Bill" or "Buffalo Bill."
He wears red shoes with a cross embroidered on the front.
Most Popes are called "Babe" because
growing up to become a Pope is a lot of fun.
All the time their bodies are becoming bigger and stranger,
but sometimes things happen to make them unhappy.
They have to go to the bathroom by themselves,
and they spend almost all of their time sleeping.
Parents seem to be incapable of helping their little Popes grow up.
Fathers tell them over and over again not to lean out of windows,
but the sky is full of them.
It looks as if they are just taking it easy,
but they are learning something else.
What, we don't know, because we are not like them.

We can't even dress like them.
We are like red bugs or mites compared to them.
We think we are having a good time cutting cartoons out of the
     paper,
but really we are eating crumbs out of their hands.
We are tiny germs that cannot be seen under microscopes.
When a Pope is ready to come into the world,
we try to sing a song, but the words do not fit the music too well.
Some of the full-bodied Popes are a million times bigger than us.
They open their mouths at regular intervals.
They are continually grinding up pieces of the cross
and spitting them out. Black flies cling to their lips.
Once they are elected they are given a bowl of cream
and a puppy clip. Eyebrows are a protection
when the Pope must plunge through dense underbrush

in search of a sheep.

REMEDY FOR BACKACHE *Judith Taylor*

While traveling in a plane coming back from seeing a married lover,
    place a tennis ball under your left buttock.
Remember your chiropractor says you're uneven, one hip hiked up,
    one pulled down.
Remember to press down on the tennis ball.
Don't remember it was he who gave it to you.
When the plane experiences turbulence, smile, what else is there to do?
Don't remember what happiness felt like.
Press down, even if it hurts.

NATURAL WOMAN *Judith Taylor*

Snails spit glistening threads on my poor pansies, chewed to lace.
Let me not hear one more rattler when I walk up the canyon!
Darwinian nineteenth century crepuscular dread overcomes me
    when the sun goes down and some *thing* scuttles in the attic.
That's a bit of a lie, but I've succeeded in saying crepuscular.
You could say I've a yes/no relationship with nature.
Sunning themselves on the patio, geckos, of whom I'm fond, do
    insouciant push-ups.
I swoosh my broom around, a warning to centipedes oozing their way
    across the carpet.
This is the deal: we all stay where we belong, and no one gets hurt.

MISTAKES *Judith Taylor*

As he put me on the train to college, Father said, Don't make any
  mistakes.
I became the Princess of Mistakes.
The interesting thing about looking out a window—it tells the truth, but
  only one truth.
All vision is blandishment, I didn't know that then.
Someone was always saying, Don't Touch.
One of my more persistent mistakes: not knowing why I couldn't have
  everything I wanted.
Everything can be changed into everything, I heard another ten-year-
  old say.

INSTRUCTIONS TO HER NEXT HUSBAND *Judith Taylor*

What shall I put in my experimental trousseau?
A paint box, a pint of scotch, a box of chocolates.
A set of masks with pleasant expressions.
Instructions on how to bow and curtsey, dance the reel.
I don't want any smoldering hotcakes for breakfast.
No indigo looks either, take some pills instead.
If you see me staring out the window, tiptoe past wearing a bear's
  head.

273

NAOLA BEAUTY ACADEMY, NEW ORLEANS, 1945 *Natasha Trethewey*

Made hair? The girls here
put a press on your head
last two weeks. No naps.

They learning. See the basins?
This where we wash. Yeah,
it's hot. July jam.

Stove always on. Keep the combs
hot. Lee and Ida bumping hair
right now. Best two.

Ida got a natural touch.
Don't burn nobody.
Her own's a righteous mass.

Lee, now she used to sew.
Her fingers steady
from them tiny needles.

She can fix some bad hair.
Look how she lay them waves.
Light, slight, and polite.

Not a one out of place.

HISTORY LESSON *Natasha Trethewey*

I am four in this photograph, standing
on a wide strip of Mississippi beach,
my hands on the flowered hips

of a bright bikini. My toes dig in,
curl around wet sand. The sun cuts
the rippling Gulf in flashes with each

tidal rush. Minnows dart at my feet
glinting like switchblades. I am alone
except for my grandmother, other side

of the camera, telling me how to pose.
It is 1970, two years after they opened
the rest of this beach to us,

forty years since the photograph
where she stood on a narrow plot
of sand marked *colored*, smiling,

her hands on the flowered hips
of a cotton meal-sack dress.

YVETTE MIMIEUX IN *HIT LADY* *David Trinidad*

All I remember is she drives a red
sports car and wears an ankh around her neck
and is instructed by The Company
to bump off some union bigwig because
he's scheduled to testify against a
Mafioso so she assumes a new
identity and starts dating him and
naturally he falls madly in love
with her not suspecting that this pert blonde
sitting on the other side of the pink
roses at the fancy restaurant is
actually the best assassin in
the business but when the time comes to pull
the trigger she breaks out in a cold sweat
and can't go through with it because all she
really wants is to quit The Company
and marry her struggling artist boyfriend
who's played by Dack Rambo and who of course
has no idea she kills people for a
living so she slips away and puts her
silencer in a storage locker at
the airport and flies to this picturesque
seaside village in Mexico where Dack
paints his unsalable masterpieces
and hoping to make a fresh start she tells
him everything but it turns out that Dack
works for The Company too so he shoots
her in the back on the beach and she dies.

DOUBLE TROUBLE *David Trinidad*

· ·

Patty:

"Hi, Mom! I'm home!"
I shouted as I burst
through the front door.
"Hello, dear." I dashed
upstairs, threw my books
on the floor, tossed
on a stack of singles
and flopped down on
the bed. Chad & Jeremy
sent me instantly to
Dreamsville. I rolled
over and reached for
my princess phone. "Hi,
Sue Ellen." "HI! Oh,
Patty!" she gushed,
"You're absolutely the
talk of the campus! I
mean you're practically
a celebrity!" We gig-
gled about how I'd
been dragged to the
principal's office
for cutting my geome-
try class and spying
on Richard in the
boys' locker room.
"Have you told your
dad yet?" "And miss
my date with Richard
tonight? Not on your
life! I'm meeting him
at the Shake Shop at
eight." There was a
knock on my door. "I
gotta run, Sue Ellen.
See you tomorrow." We

Cathy:

From the beginning, I
was opposed to Patty's
"wild" idea. It just
didn't seem feasible.
Her enthusiasm, how-
ever, was dizzying.
After listening to her
plan, she persuaded
me to exchange clothes
with her. Frantically,
she threw on my white
blouse, plaid skirt,
knee socks and oxfords
while, reluctantly, I
slipped into her sweat
shirt, blue jeans and
scruffy tennis shoes.
Next, she brushed her
flip into a pageboy
and wiped the makeup
off her face, then
spun around, brushed
my pageboy into a flip
and applied her fa-
vorite Yardley shade
(Liverpool Pink) to my
pursed lips. We stood
back and looked at each
other in the mirror. It
was perfectly uncanny:
I couldn't even tell us
apart. Patty squealed
with delight and grabbed
my hands. "Now, Cath,"
she coached, "Try not
to act so brainy, or

277

hung up. "Come in!" It was Dad. I'd never seen him look so mad. "I received a call from the principal of your school today," he said. My heart just about stopped. "Gosh, Pop-O . . ." "Don't 'Gosh, Pop-O' me, young lady. *You* are grounded. For the next two weeks, you're to stay home and study every night. You're to be in bed by nine o'clock. No phone privileges." "OH!" I cried. "No music." He switched off the phonograph. "And clean up this mess!" The door slammed behind him. I moaned and buried my head in the pillow. My whole life was ruined! What about my date??? How in the world could I be in two places at once? Just then, Cathy came into the room. "Hello, Patty," she smiled. I stared at her. She blinked back. "Anything wrong?" "Yes! No! I mean LIKE WOW!" I yelled as I jumped up and down. "I have the *wildest* idea!!!"

we'll never pull this off!" She picked up a few library books and said "Bye-eee," then glided out the door. I sat down and studied for my geometry midterm. At one point, Ross stuck his head in the room. "What's up, Sis?" he asked. I took a deep breath, turned around and said "Scram, brat!" in the harshest tone of voice I could muster. He made a nasty face and stomped off. The real test came at nine o'clock, when Uncle Martin stopped by to turn out the lights. "I hope you understand this is for your own good," he said. "I dig, Pop-O," I uttered with a weak smile. He didn't seem the least bit suspicious, so I slid into Patty's bed and blew a goodnight kiss at him. Then, for a convincing finishing touch, I blew another kiss across the room, at Patty's heart-shaped framed photograph of Frankie Avalon.

WHAT WE COULD DO *William Trowbridge*

"What shall we ever do?"
—The Waste Land

Late tonight, when Sears or Penney's
or Wal-Mart or even Monkey Ward
wouldn't give us the time of day,
we could dial up L. L. Bean,
bring that voice, bright and infallible
as a tuning fork, into our doubt-strafed,
harshly lighted homes to grant our wish
for a Shepherd's Check Flannel Shirt,
or, if they're out of stock, a pair
of Bolle Irex Aviator Sportglasses,
or, a pair of Helly-Hansen Lifa Prolite
Underwear. We can't afford to be
too choosy, so maybe we could ask *them*
to pick out something nice, a surprise
to lift us from what we call our neighborhood,
that mile-wide miss we still can't quite believe,
and drop us into the shrink-resistant heart
of some coastal woodscape: Look! Down there!
It's our springer spaniel, our teal-green rucksack,
our Easy-Pitch Geodesic Tent with vestibule!

O PARADISE *William Trowbridge*

Maybe it isn't choirs of cherubim with perfect pitch
or lions snuggling up with lambs and shepherds. Maybe
it's something like a friend and I once saw,
looking in his basement window when we were shy
with zits and stumble bones. There was my friend's
big brother with a girl and his own motorcycle, a candy-apple
Triumph with red-orange flames along the tank and chrome pipes
wide enough for Charlemagne to hear. Yes, there he was,
sitting by the furnace, with girl *and* motorcycle, his hands
dark with gear oil and expertise, and hers the same,
so that if they kissed, and they did, they had to hold
their hands away, as dancers might—a *pas de deux*
by Kelly and Caron.
                              One kiss, then back to bolts
and sprockets for a while; then later, I supposed,
the two of them astride that friendly beast.

                                            And there
we were, outside, about to pedal into another
Friday night, toward the football game, where cheerleaders
lifted up their arms, which lifted up their breasts,
and kicked the cold October air for love.

CURTAIN CALL *William Trowbridge*

At last they stand together, flushed,
reborn, bathed in our applause: York,
Clarence, Ann, the little princes, and,
all self-effacing smiles, Richard himself,
gone straight as anyone, an actor like the rest,
who now hold hands with him, all as fresh
from mocking death as the magician's helper
who leapt before us from the hilt encrusted box
or our father, who, the time his corpse act
got too real for us, raised his head and grinned.
For a moment it seems he might be here,
on stage with the others, with our mother,
with a whole growing cast of those we loved
or didn't, still in makeup and costume
to show the wounds, the sicknesses are void,
the years imaginary. We grin like fools,
smack our hands together till they sting.

TERMINATION *Fred Voss*

Feeling the vibrations coming out of the machines
with his palm flat against them,
and leaning his good ear
close to the green sides of the machines,
listening for the gears and shafts
turning in the guts of the machines,
listening for things only he
knew to listen for,
the foreman's whole body was aware
as the machines poured their decades of secrets
into his hand and ear
and he knew,
he knew what would happen to each of them,
whether there would be an accident
or whether it was alright.
His hands and jaw trembled slightly
from the 25 years
of the roars and shudders and chatterings
of steel mill drop hammers and presses and grinding wheels,
but he was still strong.

But the new hotshot manager and the machine operator
who wanted to be foreman
were into speed,
and the foreman took too long with his hand and ear
trying to keep machine cutters from blowing up in operators' faces,
so they rode him
until
each morning when he came to work and put his hardhat on
there seemed to be a heavier weight on his head,
pushing him into the concrete floor
of the steel mill,
driving his neck and his head
down into his shoulders
as if he were a shaft being driven down through concrete
by a jackhammer,
the trembling growing in his fingers
and jaws

until he had a stroke
that stopped the trembling and him
for good.

That manager and machine operator
really knew how to get the job done.

THE STUD *Fred Voss*

He had worked out at Gold's Gym
until he could bench-press 450 pounds.

He walked around the machine shop
waving a 50-pound lead hammer above his head

with one hand,
and his hammer blows
echoed off the machine shop walls
like gunshots.

Then he started talking
about how much he liked to fuck
his boyfriend.

For the first time in the machine shop's 20-year history,
no one was telling any faggot jokes.

SUN WORSHIPER *Fred Voss*

It always made me feel better
to see the sunlight
as I worked in the steel mill,
I'd look up at the plastic windows in the 100-foot-high wall
to see it
whenever I could as I
stood on the cold concrete floor and gripped the cold
blocks of steel and machine handles and I'd
feel especially good
when a shaft of that sunlight pointed
down through a high window
to strike the concrete floor or
my machine I'd stand in the shaft of light
it was
magic on my skin, it was hope
as I tried to make it through another 8 hours,
I'd be drunk with the sunlight on my skin
and I'd walk out on the asphalt
along the tin wall outside the steel mill
to stand in the sunlight and stare at it burning
on the asphalt all around my shadow until I believed
that I wasn't my shadow at all
but rather the sunlight
all around it.

AT THE ST. LOUIS INSTITUTE OF MUSIC *Ronald Wallace*

When Mr. Croxford
flicked his skinny wrist,
and the metronome began
its slow tick in his throat,
I knew that I was lost.
My thick hands tripped and stumbled
over the deviant keys,
my sour stomach off-key,
out of tune.
Outside, the day grew taut,
the fall air thin as wire,
and his voice, that cracked
and raspy sounding board,
sent me home.

All week I'd hear him clicking
out in center field, as
bases loaded, I'd pop up.
Or in the lunchroom,
flirting with the girls,
I'd feel his thin wrist
measuring my tongue until
his cracked voice rasped me back
and there I'd be again, legs
dangling from the stool,
wishing I had practiced.

Until one day they caught him
in the washroom
in a stall with Porky Brown,
and my short unhappy practice sessions ended.
I can't say I wasn't glad, or that
I felt much pity for him:
I made first string and several girls
and easily forgot him.

Yet, years later, safely married,
on days flat and diminished,
as I practice my profession
in the silence of my room,
I miss the crazy bastard,
and wish him back to abuse me
into song.

A HOT PROPERTY *Ronald Wallace*

. . . .

I am not. I am
an also-ran,
a bridesmaid, a finalist,
a second-best bed. I am
the one they could just
as easily have given it to
but didn't.
I'm a near miss, a close second,
an understudy, a runner-up.
I'm the one who was just
edged, shaded, bested, nosed out.
I made the final cut,
the short list,
the long deliberation.
I'm good, very good,
but I'm not good enough.
I'm an alternate, a backup,
a very close decision,
a red ribbon, a handshake,
a glowing commendation.
You don't know me.
I've a dozen names,
all honorably mentioned.
I could be anybody.

IN A PIG'S EYE *Ronald Wallace*

I am a male chauvinist pig,
they say. Suddenly, I am
snuffling and grunting, my long tongue wallowing.
"Week-week! Week!" I say.
See? I don't take them seriously,
they say. No men take them
seriously. Suddenly I am
sober as stone. Deep wrinkles chiseled
in my brow. I could not crack
a joke if I wanted to and I don't.
See? I am impassive. I don't listen,
they say. Suddenly I sprout ears,
ears on my head, down my neck,
back, arms, and legs, until I am
all ears. See? I'm not serious,
they say. I am two-faced. Suddenly
while my one face nods its stone head
my other face snorts off toward the kitchen,
its snout full of aprons and babies.
See? I don't take them seriously,
they say. I keep sticking myself in
where I'm not wanted. I'm a real prick,
they say. Suddenly I am
blushing, filling with blood, until
I decide it's time to stand up for myself.
See? I'm about to spout off again.
I'm so predictable, they say.

CONSTIPATION *Ronald Wallace*

Stuck each summer at Bible camp
with the ten-year-old wits and prophets,
I would not be
the victim of hoots and whistles,
the object of chortles and leers.
I knew the body was holy.
So, chary of farts and gasses,
I squeezed it back all week,
and learned the proper responses:
He who smelt it, dealt it;
A skunk can't smell his own stink.

Until one night,
cramped up and desperate,
I sneaked out to the latrine,
and there saw Sally Harper,
immaculate in the moonlight,
angelic as a dream,
slide through the forbidden door
as the night filled with her
blats, toots, grunts, and raspberries.
And then I laughed myself silly,
and knew what a heaven was for.

THE SINGER *Chocolate Waters*

She lives in the apartment below me.
At least I think she lives there.
I have never actually seen her.
Maybe just her voice lives there
and she moved out years ago.
In New York no one knows the difference
as long as the rent is paid.
The Singer has several unusual styles of singing,
depending on how late at night it is,
how depressed she is or how drunk she is.
None of her styles depend on whether
I want to listen to her.
In her 60s Rock Band mode she imagines she's Janis Joplin.
Unfortunately, she's more off-key than Janis ever was,
and she needs about two more quarts of Southern Comfort.
Or maybe I need two more quarts.
In her Contemporary Pop mode she turns into Twisted Sister
and Liza: "If I can make it there, I'll make it anywhere.
It's up to you New York, New York," she screams.
I open the window, "So make it already and move to another
    building!"
In her Judy Collins mode she can actually sing.
At least she does it quietly enough to make me think so.
There's an older man who goes in and out of her apartment.
He looks like John Gotti.
My kinder self says maybe he's her father.
I wish he was John Gotti.
Then he could throw us all a party
and I'd be so busy eating steak
I wouldn't care if she sang or not.
To tell the truth I think I met her the other day.
She was with that man who looks like John Gotti.
Our eyes locked momentarily.
"The Singer?" I asked tentatively.
She shook her head in agreement.
"I live in the apartment just above you."
"Ahhh," she nodded knowingly,
"The Writer."

You've been walking through
a huge hat shop for years.
Hats are everywhere, every
kind of hat. But you aren't

allowed to touch more than
a few, and most of those,
you aren't allowed to try.
And of those few you are

allowed to try, not one fits
right. But all the while
Time hovers over you,
a gray-haired haberdasher,

muttering "Come on,
come on," until you finally
shut your eyes and grope
around until you find one

you can touch, and which
you can get on your head,
and you declare in a loud
voice "I love this one!"

And then you pay, and put
it on, and walk outside
praying that, like leather,
it fits better with time.

BIBLICAL ALSO-RANS *Charles Harper Webb*

Hanoch, Pallu, Hezron, Carmi,
Jemuel, Ohad, Zohar, Shuni:
one Genesis mention's all you got.

Ziphion, Muppim, Arodi: lost
in a list even the most devout skip over
like small towns on the road to L.A.

How tall were you, Shillim?
What was your favorite color, Ard?
Did you love your wife, Iob?

Not even her name survives.
Adam, Eve, Abel, Cain—
these are the stars crowds surge to see.

Each hour thousands of Josephs,
Jacobs, Benjamins are born.
How many Oholibamahs? How many

Mizzahs draw first breath today?
Gatam, Kenaz, Reuel? Sidemen
in the band. Waiters who bring

the Perignon and disappear.
Yet they loved dawn's garnet light
as much as Moses did. They drank

wine with as much delight.
I thought my life would line me up
with Samuel, Isaac, Joshua.

Instead I stand with Basemath, Hoglah,
Ammihud. Theirs are the names
I honor; theirs, the deaths I feel,

their children's tears loud as any
on the corpse of Abraham, their smiles
as missed, the earth as desolate

without them: Pebbles on a hill.
Crumbs carried off by ants.
Jeush. Dishan. Nahath. Shammah.

AMPLIFIED DOG *Charles Harper Webb*

"What's that?!" hisses my wife.
I hear, through thick layers of sleep,
a voice outside. Distorted. Blaring.

I shuffle to the window. Full moon gleams
on the blue plastic I spread to funnel off
El Niño rains. The night is still.

My feet leak heat. I'm moving back to bed
when the voice starts to sing. In Spanish.
Amplified. By what—a blown-out stereo?

"Should we call the cops?" my wife whispers.
"No. It's nothing," I say. Then the dog
speaks: Woof!—distorted like the song.

A scene tunes in: A man swigging Cuervo Gold.
His wife, Dalila's, gone. His heart hurts,
so he pulls out the P.A. he's kept since he sang

in Los Pochos, back when he met her.
Maybe she'll hear him from Ramon's,
four blocks away. Maybe she'll throw on her clothes

while Ramon, belly swaying in boxers,
can't hold her back. But no.
She doesn't come. So the man lets Paco in.

Tail-wagging Paco: man's best friend.
"She loved you more than me," he says,
and sets the mike to Paco's height. "Call her, boy."

Paco sniffs the mike, then barks, and hears
his voice—Woof!—louder than it's ever been.
How many times has he stood in the yard straining

to warn people how much they're screwing up?
Woof! Woof! all day. But they won't hear.
They never learn. Hector, as usual, passes out.

Hector—his friend, who couldn't smell trouble
when Dalila reeked of it. Poor Hector, stupid and sad,
just like a man. So Paco calls his warning

as the moon tunnels through black night to silver sky.
Woof! *The world you've made stinks to high heaven.*
Woof! *You're mean to one another.*

Woof! *You let bad people lead you.* Woof!
*You work too much. You waste your time
on trivialities.* Woof! *Even sex is work for you.*

Paco loves the way his voice rattles the house,
then flies off in all directions
like pigeons when he runs right into them.

"If it's nothing," my wife says, "come back to bed."
"Quiet," I growl under my breath.
"I'm listening, Paco. Tell me everything."

YOU DON'T WANT TO HEAR A POEM, DO YOU? *Don Weinstock*

This isn't a very good poem.

I probably shouldn't read it to you.

It's not really very interesting,

        except maybe to me.

Everybody will be bored by it.

I hope you'll forgive me for reading it.

I know I shouldn't keep talking about myself.

I just wrote it down.

It still needs a lot of work.

Sorry.

BLACK SLIP *Terry Wolverton*

She told me she had always fantasized
about a woman in a black slip.
It had to do with Elizabeth Taylor
in "Butterfield 8."

She came to my house with a huge box
gift-wrapped with gigantic ribbons.
Inside, a black slip.
Slinky, with lace across the bodice.
She told me how she was embarrassed
in the department store,
a woman in men's pants
buying a black slip clearly not intended for herself,
and about the gay men in line behind her,
sharing the joke.

She asked me to try it on.
I took it into the bathroom, slipped it over my head.
I stared at myself for a long time
before I came out of the bathroom
walked over to her
lying on the bed.

That was the first time. It got easier.
The black slip was joined by a blue slip
then a red one
then a long lavender negligee, the back slit to there.

I wore them to bed.
In the morning she would smile and say
how much she loved waking up next to a woman in a slip.
The black slip remained our favorite.
We always made love when I wore the black slip.

Once I showed up at her door late at night
wearing a long coat
with only the black slip underneath.

One night I cooked dinner at her apartment
wearing nothing but the black slip
and red suede high heels.

It was always the first thing to pack when we went on vacation.

And she used to make me promise
that if we ever broke up
I'd never wear that slip for anyone else.

I don't know where it is now.

Stripped of that private skin
when we broke up
I never went back to claim it.

I think she must have
packed it
given it
thrown it
away.

On bad days I imagine her
sliding it over the head of some new love
whispering about Elizabeth Taylor
and waking up to a woman in a slip.

Or perhaps
it's still there
draped on the back of the door.

A sinuous shadow.

A moan in the dark.

THE BUSINESS OF LOVE IS CRUELTY *Dean Young*

It scares me, the genius we have
for hurting one another. I'm seven,
as tall as my mother kneeling and
she's kneeling and somehow I know

exactly how to do it, calmly,
enunciating like a good actor projecting
to the last row, shocking the ones
who've come in late, cowering

out of their coats, sleet still sparking
on their collars, a voice nearly licking
their ears above the swordplay and laments:
I hate you.

Now her hands are rising to her face.
Now the fear done flashing through me,
I wish I could undo it, take it back,
but it's a question of perfection,

carrying it through, climbing the steps
to my room, chosen banishment, where
I'll paint the hair of my model
Bride of Frankenstein purple and pink,

heap of rancor, vivacious hair
that will not die. She's rejected
of course her intended, cathected
the desires of six or seven bodies

onto the wimp Doctor. And Herr Doktor,
what does he want among the burning villages
of his proven theories? Well, he wants
to be a student again, free, drunk,

making the cricket jump, but
his distraught monster's on the rampage
again, lead-footed, weary, a corrosive
and incommunicable need sputtering

his chest, throwing oil like a fouled-up
motor: how many times do you have to die
before you're dead?

CHAPPED LIPS *Dean Young*

The problem with childhood
is it's wasted on children.
Look at them all strung together
not being run over by the bus.
They're not nearly scared enough.
Just look how they color,
they think they'll be Matisses forever.
They think you can just get up in the morning
and put on velvet shoes. And they're small,
if they were any smaller you could stick them
to the ceiling like flies but no,
they keep lofting back down
like defeated balloons
but what do they know of defeat?
What do they know of the broken bathysphere?
In their little mittens and hats,
truly they look absorbent,
but just try using one to wipe up a spill
and there are so many spills:
spills that make ducks sick,
spills that dissolve railroads,
spills we don't even know what they're doing
but they're sure doing it.
Try explaining that to a child
and all you get is la la la.
Try getting one to sit for an hour
with her face in her hands.
They have almost nothing to remember
so what they forgive could be forgiven
by anyone. They don't pay taxes.
They're completely devoid of pubic hair.

THE WRECKERS *Rafael Zepeda*

At night they cross the border,
brown men in brown trucks
with brown windows.
They are covered with dust.
Their diesel puffs behind them.
And it is strange that their
white license plates say
FRONT on the front
and FRONT on the back.
Just before dawn they find the
old buildings. The doors open,
the brown men get out,
crow bars in their right hands,
hammers at their sides.
Behind them comes a hunchback
with the sledge hammers.

I watched them take Beacon Street
in Pedro, the old Long Beach Municipal.
I watched them take Spanish Mansions from
along the ocean, and one place that
some Bauhaus guy probably designed.
They take the chrome rails, the fixtures,
the doors, the plumbing, the bricks
and all the big lumber. The supports.
They rip up the plaster, the dust rising.
They gut the places and knock them down;
then there's an empty dirt lot,
high rise material.

But now I have the feeling
that one day
I will go south
to the land of the quetzal bird
and there they'll be
the old buildings that they took,
Beacon Street set up along the coast

at the Sea of Cortez Historical Museum,
and the old Municipal,.
renowned for when the Band played there,
alongside of it.
The mansions and the chrome-covered buildings.
Everything.
Because they're taking things back,
piece by piece.
Taking California, Arizona, New Mexico, Texas,
Nevada, Colorado and Utah.
As much as they can get.
And one day they'll have it all
down there.

THE PHILOSOPHICAL EMANCIPATION *Rafael Zepeda*

We are on the roof today
laying fiberglass shingles
and Steve Parisi, who is younger than I,
but much more experienced
is measuring the lap with his hammer.
My hammer is makeshift
an old axe I once used as a tomahawk
when my father wasn't looking.

I look down my line of shingles
and see that it waves.
Beyond the wave rise the palm trees
for the half mile to the beach.
They're straighter than my line is.

So I ask Steve, "You know, I think
I'd better rip these up. Look at them."
He stands with his roofing hammer in his hand
and looks down the line.
"Don't worry about it," he says.
"Roofing is not an exact art."

LIVING WITH OTHERS *Al Zolynas*

—For Arlie

Yesterday, I discovered my wife
often climbs our stairs on all fours.

In my lonely beastliness,
I thought I was alone,
the only four-legged climber, the forger
of paths through thickets to Kilimanjaro's summit.

In celebration then, side by side,
we went up the stairs on all our fours,
and after a few steps
our self-consciousness slid from us
and I growled low in the throat
and bit with blunt teeth my mate's shoulder and
she laughed low
in her throat,
and rubbed her haunches on mine.

At the top of the stairs
we rose on our human feet
and it was fine and fitting somehow;
it was Adam and Eve rising
out of themselves before the Fall—
or after; it was survivors on a raft
mad-eyed with joy
rising to the hum of a distant rescue.

I live for such moments.

THE WAY HE'D LIKE IT *Al Zolynas*

Let me be the man who
walking among tall trees
is struck by lightning,
but is not killed;
who somersaults in a cloud
fizzing with burnt hair
and lands on his feet, shoes smoking,
and shakes his head saying,
"Jesus, that smarts!"

Let me be the man
hit by the last ash
of a dissolving meteorite.
Let it light on my head
like a benediction.

Let me be the man who walks
away from shipwrecks.

In a leveled city,
let me be the man found
17 days later under a former
insurance building sucking
air through the plumbing saying,
"I never really thought of giving up."

From all disasters let me rise
wholly. On my face,
let me have beautiful dueling scars.

THE SAME AIR *Al Zolynas*

—For Guy Murchie,
The Seven Mysteries of Life

the same air
that moves
through me and you
through the waving branches
of the bronchial tree
through veins
through the heart
the same air
that fills balloons
that carries voices
full of lies and truths
and half-truths
that holds up the wings of butterflies
humming birds eagles hang gliders 747s
the same air
that sits like a dull relative
on humid lakes
in Minnesota in summer
the same air
trapped in vintage champagne
in old bicycle tires lost tennis balls
the air inside a vial in a sarcophagus
in a tomb in a pyramid
buried beneath the sand
the same air
inside your freezer
wrapping its cold arms
around your t.v. dinners
the same air that supports you
that supports me
the same air that moves through us
that we move through
the same air frogs croak with
cattle bellow with
monks meditate with and on

the same air we moan with
in pleasure or in pain
the breath I'm taking now
will be in China in two weeks
my lungs have passed an atom
of oxygen that passed through the lungs
of Socrates or Plato
or Lao-tsu or Buddha
or Walt Disney or the President
or a starving child in Somalia
or certainly you
you right here right now
yes certainly you
the same air
the very same air

The new grass, the new lambs
eating the grass, the new calves
butting heads under the slow gaze
of bull-fathers beyond wire fences,
the sparrows flying with pieces of straw
in their beaks, the seagulls a thousand
miles from salt water eating worms
turned up by the plow,
the earth itself . . .
                    It is not enough.
I go into the house and put on
Beethoven's 6th symphony, the *Pastorale.*
I listen to violins and oboes,
former trees, pretending to be winds,
birds and brooks. I listen to drums,
the hides of animals, trying to be
thunder.
                    It all works, somehow:
the thunder, controllable—a living room
thunder, and yet the living room a world, too.
Outside, the earth is being lifted
by the music, it is rising
out of itself, trees wave their arms
like mad conductors, the sky is breaking
into applause.

ACKNOWLEDGMENTS

Special thanks to Suzanne Lummis, Ron Koertge, and Gerry Locklin for
many contributions to the theory and practice of Stand Up poetry.

Kim Addonizio: "What the Dead Fear," © 1994 by Kim Addonizio.
Reprinted from *The Philosopher's Club*, poems by Kim Addonizio, with
the permission of BOA Editions, Ltd. "For Desire," © 2000 by Kim
Addonizio. Reprinted from *Tell Me*, poems by Kim Addonizio, with the
permission of BOA Editions, Ltd.

Jack Anderson. "Going to Norway," © Jack Anderson. Reprinted by
permission of the author.

Ginger Andrews: "The Housewife," "Evidently, She Says," "Prayer," and
"O That Summer" from *An Honest Answer*, © 1999 by Ginger Andrews.
Reprinted by permission of Story Line Press (storylinepress.com).

John Balaban: "At 4:00 A.M. Asleep" and "Words for My Daughter" from
Locusts at the Edge of Summer: New and Selected Poems, © 1997 by John
Balaban. Reprinted by permission of Copper Canyon Press, P.O. Box 271,
Port Townsend, WA 98368-0271, USA.

Dorothy Barresi: "Bad Joke" first appeared in *Crab Orchard Review*. "Glass
Dress" first appeared in *Kenyon Review*. Both poems © Dorothy Barresi,
reprinted by permission of the author.

Dinah Berland: "Blazon," © 2001 by Dinah Berland. Reprinted by
permission of the author.

Laurel Ann Bogen: "Pygmy Headhunters and Killer Apes, My Lover and
Me" from *Rag Tag We Kiss*, published by Illuminati, © 1989 by Laurel
Ann Bogen. "I Eat Lunch with a Schizophrenic" and "Havana" from
The Burning: New and Selected Poems 1970–1990, published by Red Wind
Books, © 1991 by Laurel Ann Bogen. Reprinted by permission of the
author.

Laure-Anne Bosselaar: "English Flavors," © 1997 by Laure-Anne Bosselaar.
Reprinted from *The Hour Between Dog and Wolf*, poems by Laure-Anne
Bosselaar, with the permission of BOA Editions, Ltd.

Catherine Bowman: "No Sorry" and "Demographics," © Catherine
Bowman. Reprinted by permission of the author.

Kurt Brown: "Money As Water" and "Return of the Prodigals" from *Return
of the Prodigals*, © 2000 by Kurt Brown. Reprinted by permission of
Four Way Books, New York, NY.

Stephanie Brown: "Chapter One," "Allegory of the Supermarket," and
"Agapé" from *Allegory of the Supermarket*, published by the University

Philip Dacey: "Form Rejection Letter" from *How I Escaped from the Labyrinth and Other Poems*, published by Carnegie Mellon University Press, © 1977 by Philip Dacey. "Coke" and "Squeak" from *Night Shift at the Crucifix Factory*, published by the University of Iowa Press, © 1991 by Philip Dacey. "The Rules" from *The Man with Red Suspenders*, published by Milkweed Editions, © 1986 by Philip Dacey. Reprinted by permission of the author.

Jim Daniels: "Blessing the House" and "The Hoagie Scam" from *Blessing the House*, by Jim Daniels, © 1997. Reprinted by permission of the University of Pittsburgh Press.

Stephen Dobyns: "Confession" from *Body Traffic* by Stephen Dobyns, published by Viking Penguin, a division of Penguin Books USA Inc., © 1990 by Stephen Dobyns. "Pony Express" and "How to Like It" from *Cemetery Nights* by Stephen Dobyns, Viking Penguin, a division of Penguin Books USA Inc., © 1987 by Stephen Dobyns. Reprinted by permission of the author.

Denise Duhamel: "I'm Dealing with My Pain" from *The Star-Spangled Banner* by Denise Duhamel, © 1999 by Denise Duhamel. Reprinted by permission of the publisher, Southern Illinois University Press. "Why, on a Bad Day, I Can Relate to the Manatee" from *Smile!*, published by Warm Spring Press, © 1993 by Denise Duhamel. Reprinted by permission of the author. "Ego" from *Queen for a Day: Selected and New Poems*, by Denise Duhamel, © 2001. Reprinted by permission of the University of Pittsburgh Press. "Buddhist Barbie" from *Kinky*, Orchises Press, © 1997 by Denise Duhamel. Reprinted by permission of the author.

Stephen Dunn: "The Shame Place" from *Local Time*, published by William Morrow & Co., © 1986 by Stephen Dunn. Reprinted by permission of the author. "On Hearing the Airlines Will Use a Psychological Profile to Catch Potential Skyjackers" and "At the Smithville Methodist Church," from *New and Selected Poems: 1974–1994*, © 1994 by Stephen Dunn. Used by permission of W. W. Norton & Company, Inc.

Russell Edson: "The Retirement of the Elephant," "The Automobile," and "Ape" from *The Childhood of an Equestrian*, published by Harper & Row, © 1973 by Russell Edson. "Counting Sheep" from *The Intuitive Journey*, published by Harper & Row, © 1976 by Russell Edson. "The Categories," "Good Son Jim," "Elephant Tears," and "The Crumble-Knees" from *The Wounded Breakfast*, published by Wesleyan University Press, © 1985 by Russell Edson. Reprinted by permission of the author.

Lynn Emanuel: "The White Dress" and "The Politics of Narrative: Why I Am a Poet" from *Then, Suddenly—*, by Lynn Emanuel, © 1999. Reprinted by permission of the University of Pittsburgh Press.

Stephanie Sallaska: "To Raise the Blind on Purpose," © Stephanie Sallaska. Reprinted by permission of the author and the publishers.

Maureen Seaton: "Furious Cooking" from *Furious Cooking*, published by the University of Iowa Press, © 1996 by Maureen Seaton. "Fiddleheads" from *Little Ice Age*, published by Invisible Cities Press, © 2001 by Maureen Seaton. Reprinted by permission of the author and the publishers.

Betsy Sholl: "Monkey House" and "Four Crows at Dusk" from *Don't Explain*, winner of the 1997 Felix Pollak Prize in Poetry, © 1997. Reprinted by permission of the University of Wisconsin Press.

Joan Jobe Smith: "A Philodendron Named Joan" first appeared in *The Honeymoon of King Kong and Emily Dickinson*, published by Zerx Press, © 1993 by Joan Jobe Smith. "Honeybee upon the Tundra" and "What I Learned from the Movies," © Joan Jobe Smith. Reprinted by permission of the author.

Maura Stanton: "Drugstore Trolls" and "Revolt" from *Life Among the Trolls* published by Carnegie Mellon University Press, © 1998 by Maura Stanton. Reprinted by permission of Carnegie Mellon University Press.

Austin Straus: "All-Purpose Apology Poem" first appeared in *New Letters*, © 1984, and was anthologized in *The Maverick Poets*, © 1988 by Gorilla Press. Reprinted by permission of the author.

James Tate: "I Am a Finn," "Aunt Sophie's Morning," and "How the Pope Is Chosen," © James Tate. Reprinted by permission of the author.

Judith Taylor: "Remedy for Backache," "Natural Woman," "Mistakes," and "Instructions to Her Next Husband" are reprinted from *Curios*, by Judith Taylor, published by Sarabande Books, Inc., © 2000. Reprinted by permission of Sarabande Books.

Natasha Trethewey: "History Lesson" and "Naola Beauty Academy, New Orleans, 1945" from *Domestic Work*, published by Graywolf Press, © 2000 by Natasha Trethewey. Reprinted by permission of the author.

David Trinidad: "Double Trouble" from *Hand over Heart: Poems 1981–1988*, published by Amethyst Press, © 1991 by David Trinidad. "Yvette Mimieux in *Hit Lady*" from *Answer Song*, published by High Risk Books, © 1994 by David Trinidad. Reprinted by permission of the author.

William Trowbridge: "What We Could Do" and "O Paradise" from *O Paradise*, by William Trowbridge, © 1995 by William Trowbridge. "Curtain Call" from *Flickers*, by William Trowbridge, © 2000 by William Trowbridge. Reprinted by permission of the University of Arkansas Press.

Fred Voss: "Termination" first appeared in *Lumpen*. "Sun Worshiper" first

TITLE INDEX